MORIBYAN'S KITCHEN

CLARKSON POTTER/PUBLISHERS
NEW YORK
CLARKSONPOTTER.COM

PHOTOGRAPHS BY EVA KOLENKO

HAJAR LARBAH

MORIBYAN'S KITCHEN

100 CRAVEABLE COMFORT FOOD RECIPES

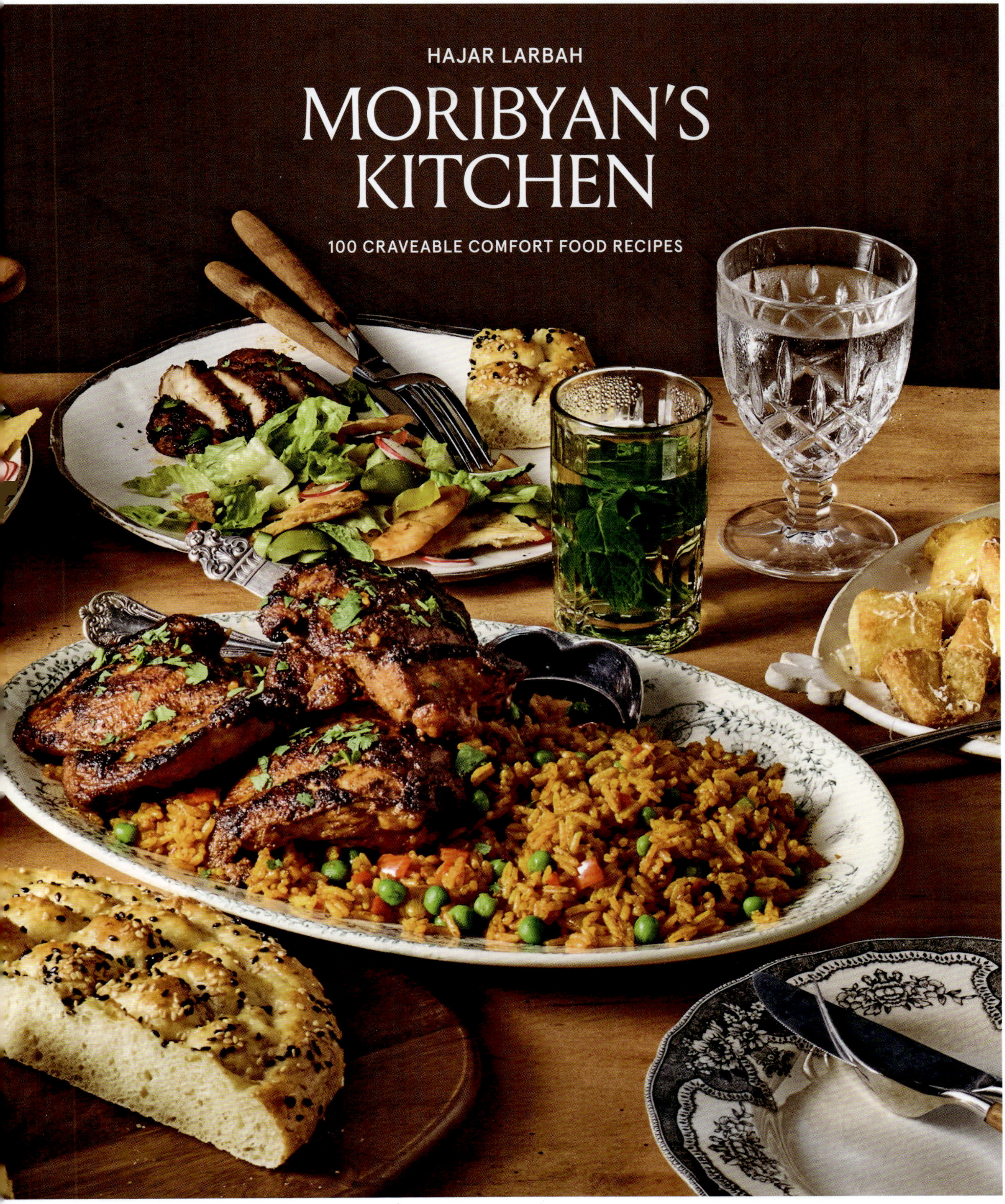

CONTENTS

The Main Event

Restaurant Remakes

All About the Bread

Sweet Treats

INTRODUCTION

In my home growing up, love wasn't always spoken in the usual three words. It was simmered in stews, folded into warm bread, and tucked into lunchboxes each morning. It was my father wandering the market in search of the ripest fruit, my mother peeling and slicing the treasures he brought home, then quietly leaving a plate on my desk while I studied. On days when the world felt heavy, my mom lifted my spirits with my favorite dish. And when I moved away for college, my sisters always sent me off with my favorite dessert, which they'd bake for me even after a long day at work, just so I'd have something sweet to remind me of home.

Food has always been the way love showed up in my family. Eid meant my mother's powdered sugar cookies that melted in your mouth. Camping meant my father's Libyan pasta, stirred with care over an open flame until the whole campsite smelled of warm spices. Picnics with friends were never complete without a North African tuna sandwich loaded with harissa. When I taste those dishes today, what comes back to me isn't only the flavor, but also the feelings of warmth around the campfire and excitement on holiday mornings.

From as early as I can remember, I was drawn to the kitchen. Being the baby of the family meant I was always at my mother's side, trailing her like a shadow. Before I ever stirred a pot, I was tagging along to the market, my small hand wrapped around hers as we moved through the busy aisles. I loved helping choose the best cuts of meat, handpicking vegetables, and sniffing bunches of herbs. My proudest moments were when I picked the perfect tomato and my mom would toss it into the bag, affirming my choice. What seemed like a simple errand at the time became my first real lesson in cooking. A meal can only be as good as the ingredients, and choosing them with care is an act of love in itself.

Back home in our kitchen, I would drag a chair to the counter to be closer to the action, peeling garlic, kneading dough, or shaping egg rolls that always came out a little lopsided. My mom never measured in teaspoons or cups; her recipes lived in her hands. Add water until the dough feels right. Stir until it thickens. Taste until it's good. She taught me that cooking wasn't about precision so much as intuition—paying attention to your senses and letting the food guide you.

That curiosity only grew every summer when my father and mother took me and my siblings to Libya and Morocco, their respective home countries. I remember sitting cross-legged on the floor outside with all my cousins, helping peel almonds for a special tea my aunt made, the air thick with the smell of roasting nuts. The room filled with laughter as my aunts told tales of the family traditions that shaped them.

INTRODUCTION

In my home growing up, love wasn't always spoken in the usual three words. It was simmered in stews, folded into warm bread, and tucked into lunchboxes each morning. It was my father wandering the market in search of the ripest fruit, my mother peeling and slicing the treasures he brought home, then quietly leaving a plate on my desk while I studied. On days when the world felt heavy, my mom lifted my spirits with my favorite dish. And when I moved away for college, my sisters always sent me off with my favorite dessert, which they'd bake for me even after a long day at work, just so I'd have something sweet to remind me of home.

Food has always been the way love showed up in my family. Eid meant my mother's powdered sugar cookies that melted in your mouth. Camping meant my father's Libyan pasta, stirred with care over an open flame until the whole campsite smelled of warm spices. Picnics with friends were never complete without a North African tuna sandwich loaded with harissa. When I taste those dishes today, what comes back to me isn't only the flavor, but also the feelings of warmth around the campfire and excitement on holiday mornings.

From as early as I can remember, I was drawn to the kitchen. Being the baby of the family meant I was always at my mother's side, trailing her like a shadow. Before I ever stirred a pot, I was tagging along to the market, my small hand wrapped around hers as we moved through the busy aisles. I loved helping choose the best cuts of meat, handpicking vegetables, and sniffing bunches of herbs. My proudest moments were when I picked the perfect tomato and my mom would toss it into the bag, affirming my choice. What seemed like a simple errand at the time became my first real lesson in cooking. A meal can only be as good as the ingredients, and choosing them with care is an act of love in itself.

Back home in our kitchen, I would drag a chair to the counter to be closer to the action, peeling garlic, kneading dough, or shaping egg rolls that always came out a little lopsided. My mom never measured in teaspoons or cups; her recipes lived in her hands. Add water until the dough feels right. Stir until it thickens. Taste until it's good. She taught me that cooking wasn't about precision so much as intuition—paying attention to your senses and letting the food guide you.

That curiosity only grew every summer when my father and mother took me and my siblings to Libya and Morocco, their respective home countries. I remember sitting cross-legged on the floor outside with all my cousins, helping peel almonds for a special tea my aunt made, the air thick with the smell of roasting nuts. The room filled with laughter as my aunts told tales of the family traditions that shaped them.

Some mornings, I'd wake before my siblings, the house still quiet, and rush downstairs to help my aunt prepare shakshuka. As the smell of stewed tomatoes and peppers filled the kitchen, she'd tell me how the same dish could taste different from city to city or even from one aunt's kitchen to another's. Each version was shaped by the region and what ingredients were available—like fish along the sea or lamb in the mountains. History shaped our cuisines, too, as ingredients and techniques introduced through colonization became interwoven with our own traditions. My summers in North Africa weren't about cooking itself but about discovering the stories that lived inside each recipe.

Back at home in California, that curiosity turned into obsession. I was glued to Food Network, filling notebooks with recipes and rushing to the kitchen to try them out. Weekends were spent baking anything that caught my interest, then bringing trays of cookies and cupcakes to school for friends to taste.

Fast-forward to my freshman year of college, when I lived hours away from family and felt homesick. I found myself turning to the kitchen even more; food was at the center of so many of my core memories, so it felt natural to want a space where I could keep those stories and recipes alive.

One afternoon, sitting in a cozy coffee shop on campus, I decided to start a food blog. I came up with the name Moribyan—a blend of the words "Moroccan" and "Libyan"—as a tribute to my parents and the cultures that shaped me. In the beginning, it was barely ten people reading along—mostly friends and family—but that was enough to keep me going. Then in 2020, Covid hit. The kitchen became a source of comfort for many, with sourdough loaves rising on counters and banana bread baking in ovens everywhere. It was more than just cooking, it was therapy: a way to quiet anxious minds and ease stress in an uncertain time. The same was true for me. Between Zoom classes (I was still in college), I started filming recipe videos for TikTok. With restaurants closed, I began posting copycat versions of the foods people were missing most. Then one video took off and what started as a small creative outlet slowly grew into a community of people bringing my recipes to life in their own kitchens.

When I think about what I want people to feel when they make my recipes, my mind goes straight to my favorite movie, *Ratatouille*. I've watched it so many times, I could recite it by heart. But one line stands out: "Anyone can cook."

Gusteau's three famous words remind me of my mom and aunts. They never once made me feel out of place in the kitchen. I could spill flour everywhere or burn something completely, and they'd still let me try again. There was never any judgment; only encouragement and a quiet trust that I'd eventually get it right.

That same spirit lives in the blog *Moribyan* and now in this book. To me, cooking is love made visible, and when you flip through these pages, my hope is that you'll feel that love in every dish you make.

About This Book

This book holds one hundred recipes, each one a little love letter. Some are to my heritage, some to the places I've traveled, and many to the everyday dishes that bring comfort. The North African dishes are closest to my heart, perfected with the help of my parents and mother-in-law. But you'll also find recipes born out of late-night cravings, childhood nostalgia, restaurant favorites, and me simply trying to make dinner faster, easier, and more delicious after a long day. There are plenty of sheet-pan meals, one-pot pastas, and thirty-minute dinners—like One-Pan Alfredo Orzo with Chicken & Spinach (page 102) and Chicken Shawarma Sheet-Pan Bake (page 131)—that prove flavor doesn't have to come with extra effort. And then there are the travel-inspired ones, like the steak frites I developed after falling in love with Paris, or the egg sandos I enjoyed from Japanese convenience stores while wandering the streets of Tokyo.

When I was growing up, my dad would bring me cookbooks from his travels, and each one felt like a window into another world. Those books taught me that a cookbook isn't just a collection of recipes; it's about discovering the stories of the people and places that shape the food we love. I loved how those pages could connect you to someone else's kitchen, even from miles away, and it made me dream of creating a book that could do the same. Because I want this book to be one you trust in your kitchen for years to come, I held every recipe to a standard beyond perfection. I tested these recipes again and again until they felt just right—some took five tries, others nine, and a few more than fifteen. (I never want to see another oatmeal creme pie again.)

In the end, all that testing was just the first chapter. The rest of the story will unfold in your hands as the pages collect the signs of a kitchen well loved: flour and oil stains, handwritten scribbles, and Post-its marking favorites. I hope every recipe in this book adds a little warmth and comfort to your days and welcomes you into the kitchen with the same open arms my mom embraced me with as a kid.

EQUIPMENT & INGREDIENTS

Equipment

You don't need a professional kitchen to cook from this book, but you will see a variety of tools that make the process easier, faster, or more fun. Whenever possible, I've given alternate methods so you can use what you already have at home. Think of this list as a mix of true essentials—like saucepans, baking sheets, a cast-iron skillet, and mixing bowls—and nice-to-haves, such as an air fryer, stand mixer, pizza steel, or blow torch. If you love baking, an investment like a stand mixer will change the game for kneading and mixing, but you'll also see hand mixer and by-hand instructions wherever possible. For gear like air fryers, blow torches, or pizza steels, I've built in backup methods, so you won't miss out on a recipe just because you don't have one specific tool.

ESSENTIALS

Baking sheets: Rimmed half-sheet pans (18 × 13 inches) are the most versatile, with a smaller 15 × 10 option handy, too. Light-colored pans are best for baking cookies, while darker ones absorb more heat and are great for roasting vegetables or potatoes. Both sizes work perfectly for sheet-pan dinners.

Casserole dish/baking dish: A large ceramic or stoneware baking dish is great for oven bakes like baked pasta, stuffed peppers, and the Strawberries & Cream Croissant French Toast Bake (page 24).

Cast-iron skillet: For perfect steaks (see page 165) and Dutch pancakes (see page 35). If you only buy one, I recommend 10 inches.

Cooling racks: Wire racks where you can rest meats, just-fried food, and more.

Dutch oven/heavy-bottomed pot: Not just for braises and stews, this is also an ideal vessel for deep-frying.

Instant-read thermometer: The best way to check meat doneness as well as oil temp for frying.

Measuring cups and spoons: Make sure to buy stackable dry measures as well as a heatproof liquid measuring cup.

Metal baking pans: You'll want two: an 8-inch square pan for Blueberry Cinnamon Crunch Coffee Cake (page 243), Almond Croissant Brown Butter Blondies (page 239), and No-Churn Fluffernutter Ice Cream (page 261); and a 9 × 13-inch pan for Cookies & Cream Tres Leches Cake (page 247).

Mixing bowls: Stackable bowls of various sizes are always useful.

Parchment paper and aluminum foil: For lining baking sheets and trays (among other things) to make cleanup easier.

Saucepans: Ideally, you'll have three: small, medium, and large. I prefer nonstick or stainless steel.

Whisk, spatula, slotted spoon: I prefer silicone for spatulas and metal for whisks and slotted spoons.

A NOTE ON MEASURING FOR BAKING

These recipes were developed using the US customary system—cups, teaspoons, and tablespoons. That said, I've also provided metric weight conversions for baking recipes (like breads and desserts), since I know many of you live outside the United States or may not have access to the same measuring cups. If you do have them, I recommend sticking with cups for the most reliable results.

I always dip the measuring cup directly into the bag or jar of flour, scoop more than you need, and then level it off with a knife. This ensures consistency and helps prevent adding too much or too little flour by accident.

NICE-TO-HAVES

Air fryer: Recipes like the Honey Buffalo Crispy Chicken Wraps (page 120) and my husband Idris's Famous Stuffed Chicken (page 135) come out perfect every time, with minimal cleanup using an air fryer. That said, I have included instructions for cooking in a conventional oven, too, so you won't miss out if you don't have one.

Blender or food processor: Great for making sauces, marinades, grinding nuts, or pulsing herbs for falafel. A food processor is usually better for chunkier textures, while a blender works well for smoother purees.

Blow torch: If you want to caramelize the sugar on your crème brûlée (see page 255) like a pro. (Although I've also provided broiler instructions.)

Cookie scooper: For perfectly portioned, uniform cookies. There are two sizes used in this book: 1½ inches for Oatmeal Creme Pies (page 235) and 2 inches for Brown Butter Chocolate Chip Cookies (page 232).

Digital scale: Great if you bake a lot and prefer to measure ingredients by weight (see A Note on Measuring for Baking, page 15).

Immersion blender: A must-have for creamy soups like Creamy Roasted Red Pepper & Tomato Soup (page 87) and Mama Nezha's Lentil Soup (page 84), this allows you to blend directly in the pot without extra dishes. It's also handy for making the hollandaise sauce for the Philly Cheesesteak Eggs Benedict (page 43). You can always use a traditional blender instead, though.

Kitchen shears: Heavy-duty kitchen or poultry shears are so useful for a million things but especially for preparing a spatchcocked chicken (see page 140).

Loaf pan: A 9 × 5-inch for the Best Banana Bread (page 240) and other quickbreads.

Pizza peel: Ideal for transferring pizza, Khachapuri (page 30), and Pita Pockets (page 227) from your workstation to a hot oven.

Pizza steel: This helps you make perfect pizzas (see page 205) with a fluffy yet crispy crust in your home oven. I personally like it more than a stone. I also use it to make Khachapuri (page 30) and Pita Pockets (page 227).

Roasting pan: To make the Spatchcocked Roast Chicken with Gravy (page 140), a roasting pan is ideal. Bonus points if it has a rack built in.

Rolling pin: To roll out any dough.

Springform pan: The best way to bake the cheesecake on page 256.

Stainless-steel vertical spit stand: This is nice to have for making Greek-Inspired Chicken Gyros (page 124). I included a DIY version but it's such a fun tool to have if you're able to get one.

Stand mixer: If you love baking, this is worth the investment. It makes kneading doughs and mixing batters so much faster and easier than doing it by hand.

Waffle maker: Just for the Brown Butter Belgian Waffles (page 39). Not all waffle makers are built the same by the way—some make thinner waffles, some make thicker Belgian-style ones. The brand I use is called Bella.

Wok: Optional but makes a huge difference with the Easiest Udon Stir-Fry with Steak (page 101).

Ingredients

This book mostly relies on ingredients you can find at a well-stocked grocery store. For the most part, you won't need anything unusual, and I've included swaps whenever possible. For a few of the more traditional North African recipes, you might need specialty ingredients like harissa or preserved lemons, but I've always found them at big supermarkets.

Baking essentials: Baking soda, baking powder, and cornstarch are key for leavening and thickening. Vanilla extract is a must for flavoring!

Butter: In most dessert recipes, I use unsalted butter; it's always my preference so I can control the salt myself. However, you can always use salted butter when there is salt in the recipe. Just lower the salt added in the recipe by ¼ teaspoon per stick.

Flour: I use all-purpose flour in most recipes, though some breads, pastries, and pizza dough may call for bread flour for better texture. In those instances, you can always use all-purpose flour in its place.

Fresh herbs: Always have a bunch of parsley and cilantro in your fridge! Some other herbs used in this book occasionally but not as commonly are basil, rosemary, thyme, dill, and mint.

Oils: Whenever neutral oil is listed, I typically opt for light olive oil or avocado oil if cooking protein or toasting something. When I'm deep-frying and list neutral oil, I prefer vegetable oil. Other options for deep-frying include canola oil, peanut oil, or safflower oil.

Pantry staples: Items like tomato paste, tomato sauce, beef and chicken broth, beans, rice, pasta, vinegars, soy sauce, and condiments (like mayo and mustard) appear in many recipes. Keeping these stocked ensures you can tackle a wide range of dishes.

Salt: Whenever a recipe mentions salt, I typically use fine sea salt for both flavor and texture. Sometimes I'll use flaky sea salt for a finishing salty and crunchy touch. Keep in mind that not all salts taste equally salty. Kosher salt, table salt, and sea salt all vary in intensity, so if you substitute one for another, you may need to adjust the amount to taste. Broths, tomato pastes, and other ingredients can also differ in saltiness depending on the brand, so always taste and adjust as you go along.

Spices: Other than salt and pepper, the ten most common spices used in this book are chili powder (the mild seasoning blend kind), paprika, garlic powder, onion powder, turmeric, cinnamon, cumin, coriander, cayenne pepper, and ginger. Some dried herbs are frequently used, such as oregano and Italian seasoning.

Sweeteners: Most recipes will call for granulated sugar, which is just plain white sugar. The next most common is brown sugar, and you can usually use light or dark interchangeably unless specified. You'll also be using powdered sugar a lot for frostings and dusting on top of desserts. Then there are sweeteners like honey and molasses, which bring their own flavor, too. In a lot of dough recipes, you can even opt for honey instead of granulated sugar.

Yeast: Instant yeast has finer granules than active dry yeast and can be mixed right into the flour, which makes it perfect for quick recipes. That said, in the recipes in this book that do use instant yeast, I still recommend a quick, ten-minute proof time, which is just an extra insurance policy to make sure your yeast wakes up properly. Active dry yeast has larger granules, needs to be dissolved in warm water first, and is often preferred in doughs that ferment slowly or chill overnight since it can develop more flavor. For the most part, you can swap them 1:1, but just remember active yeast may take a little longer to rise.

North African Ingredients

North African cooking is at the heart of who I am, and I'm so excited to share recipes that connect me to both my Libyan and Moroccan sides. I tried to pick the recipes I loved most growing up and ones I know other people will enjoy, too. I also kept this list short and sweet, with ingredients you'll actually use often and that won't be hard to find.

Lamb: Lamb is commonly used in a lot of North African dishes. A lot of recipes use lamb stew meat, which is cubed up; others use ground lamb. One recipe calls for lamb shoulder chops. The key with all lamb (except for lamb chops) is to cook it low and slow and don't stop until it's tender enough to fall apart at the touch.

Harissa: Every North African household has a jar of harissa in the fridge. This spicy chile paste is perfect for adding heat and depth to sauces (such as the harissa aioli on the Merguez-Spiced Kefta Sandwiches on page 128), salad dressings, and marinades for lamb chops. You can find it in jars at most grocery stores or even make your own (my favorite recipe is up on my blog, Moribyan.com).

Preserved lemons: These come in a jar and add a bright, tangy, and slightly fermented flavor to tagines and stews such as the Moroccan djaj mhammar (see page 117). A little goes a long way, so start with small amounts and adjust to taste.

BREAKFAST & BRUNCH

STRAWBERRIES & CREAM CROISSANT FRENCH TOAST BAKE

I'm always on the hunt for new ways to use up leftover croissants, and this bake might be the ultimate one.

Flaky croissants are stuffed with a lightly sweetened cream cheese filling and fresh strawberries, then soaked in a rich custard, and baked until golden and crisp on top but soft in the middle. It's the easiest way to feed a crowd for brunch, and the best part? You can prep it the night before and slide it straight into the oven when you wake up.

SERVES 6

- 10 ounces strawberries, hulled and chopped small
- 3 tablespoons granulated sugar
- 8 ounces cream cheese, at room temperature
- ⅓ cup powdered sugar
- 8 large croissants, either fresh or day-old

CUSTARD

- 2 large eggs
- ¾ cup half-and-half
- 3 tablespoons granulated sugar
- 1 teaspoon vanilla extract
- ¼ teaspoon ground cinnamon
- 4 tablespoons unsalted butter, cut into small cubes

FOR SERVING

- Maple syrup
- Whipped cream
- Powdered sugar

In a medium bowl, combine the strawberries and granulated sugar and let them sit for about 10 minutes to release their juices.

In a small bowl, whisk together the softened cream cheese and powdered sugar until smooth and creamy.

Slice each croissant open horizontally, keeping one side attached. Spread a layer of the cream cheese filling inside, then spoon in some of the macerated strawberries. Close the croissants and press gently to seal. Cut each croissant crosswise into about 5 pieces, keeping the hinge intact.

Arrange the croissant pieces snugly inside a 9 × 13-inch baking dish.

Make the custard: In a medium bowl, whisk together the eggs, half-and-half, granulated sugar, vanilla, and cinnamon until smooth. Pour the custard evenly over the croissants, making sure every piece is coated. Let it soak for 30 minutes. (You can also do this a day ahead and soak overnight.)

Meanwhile, preheat the oven to 350°F.

Dot the top with the butter, cover the dish with foil, and bake for 25 minutes.

Remove the foil and bake uncovered until golden, crispy, and set, 10 to 15 minutes.

Let it cool slightly, then serve warm with maple syrup, whipped cream, and a dusting of powdered sugar.

FRIED CHICKEN, EGG & CHEESE BISCUIT SANDWICHES

I used to be obsessed with Chick-fil-A's biscuit breakfast sandwiches. They were my go-to weekend pick-me-up, but there's just one problem: getting there before 10:30 a.m., when breakfast ends. As much as I'm a morning person, I'm definitely not an early breakfast person, and as a result, I've missed that cutoff more than once. One Saturday, after another failed attempt, I decided it was time to re-create my own version at home. Buttery biscuits, fluffy eggs, crispy chicken, and melty cheese come together for the ultimate homemade breakfast sandwich—no wake-up call necessary.

MAKES 6 TO 8 SANDWICHES

FRIED CHICKEN

- 2 large boneless, skinless chicken breasts
- 1 cup all-purpose flour
- ¼ cup cornstarch
- 1 tablespoon powdered sugar
- 2 teaspoons paprika
- 3 teaspoons salt
- 1½ teaspoons freshly ground black pepper
- 1 teaspoon garlic powder
- 1 teaspoon mustard powder
- ⅓ cup buttermilk
- 2 tablespoons pickle juice
- 1 large egg
- ½ teaspoon baking soda
- Neutral oil, for deep-frying

Prepare the fried chicken: Place the chicken on a cutting board and use a sharp knife to carefully slice it in half horizontally, creating two thinner pieces. (Imagine the chicken is a hamburger bun, if that helps; you're slicing it to create the top and bottom of the bun.) If it's still a bit too thick for a sandwich, cover with plastic wrap and gently pound each piece with a meat mallet or the back of a pan to even it out. From there, you can cut each piece down into smaller cutlets, about the size of your biscuit—aim for ones that are just slightly larger than the biscuit, since they'll shrink a little as they cook.

Set up a dredging station in two medium bowls: In one bowl, whisk the flour, cornstarch, powdered sugar, paprika, 2 teaspoons of the salt, 1 teaspoon of the pepper, the garlic powder, and mustard powder.

In a second bowl, whisk together the buttermilk, pickle juice, egg, baking soda, and remaining 1 teaspoon salt and ½ teaspoon black pepper. Add 3 tablespoons of the wet batter to the flour mixture and massage it with your fingers to create a shaggy and flaky texture.

Dip each chicken cutlet into the seasoned flour mixture, making sure it's fully coated. Shake off any excess, then dip it into the buttermilk/egg mixture, letting the excess drip off. Finally, return it to the flour mixture, pressing the breading firmly onto the surface so it sticks well and creates a nice, even coating. Set aside.

RECIPE & INGREDIENTS CONTINUE

Set a wire rack in a sheet pan and have near the stove. Pour 2 to 3 inches of neutral oil into a heavy-bottomed pan or Dutch oven and heat over medium heat until it registers 350°F on a deep-fry thermometer.

Working in batches to avoid overcrowding, fry the chicken until golden brown and the internal temperature reaches 165°F, 4 to 6 minutes per side. Drain the wire rack.

Assemble the sandwiches: In a medium bowl, whisk together the eggs, milk, and salt and pepper to taste.

Heat a 9-inch nonstick skillet over medium-low heat, then lightly grease it with oil. Pour in the egg mixture, spreading it evenly. Cover the skillet with a lid and cook until the eggs are set, 7 to 10 minutes, increasing the heat after 5 minutes if it seems like your eggs aren't cooking. Transfer to a cutting board and cut into squares or rounds to fit your sandwich. Place a slice of cheese on top of each egg patty while still hot so the cheese starts to melt.

Slice the warm biscuits in half crosswise. Layer each with a chicken cutlet, then an egg patty topped with a cheese slice. Serve warm and enjoy with some honey on the side, if you'd like, for drizzling.

MORIBYAN'S TIP

I like to steam the eggs so they set into a fluffy patty you can slice into perfect rounds or squares, but if you're in a rush, a quick scramble or fried egg totally works, too.

ASSEMBLY

6 large eggs
¼ cup whole milk
Salt and freshly ground black pepper
1½ teaspoons neutral oil
6 to 8 American or cheddar cheese slices (1 per sandwich)
6 to 8 Melt-in-Your-Mouth Biscuits (page 215), warm
Honey (optional)

KHACHAPURI
(Georgian Cheese Bread)

The first time I made this traditional savory pastry from Georgia (the country, not the US state!), I couldn't believe how easy it was. Shape dough into ovals, pinch the edges to form a rim, and fill with cheese. At the end, crack an egg into the center and bake just until the yolk is barely set. When it comes out, rip off pieces of crust to dip into the bubbling, cheesy center. It's crispy on the outside, molten in the middle, and truly one of those recipes that leaves you speechless after the first bite.

MAKES 3 BREADS TO SERVE 4 TO 6

- 1½ cups shredded mozzarella cheese
- 1½ cups whole-milk ricotta cheese
- 1½ cups crumbled feta cheese
- All-purpose flour, for dusting
- 15 ounces pizza dough, homemade (see page 205) or store-bought
- Egg wash: 1 egg, well whisked
- 3 large eggs
- 3 tablespoons unsalted butter
- Flaky sea salt and freshly ground black pepper, for garnish

Adjust a rack to the lowest position and preheat the oven to 450°F with a pizza steel (see Tips) on the rack. Let it preheat for 30 minutes.

In a medium bowl, mix together the mozzarella, ricotta, and feta.

Lightly flour a clean work surface. Divide the dough into three 5-ounce pieces. Roll out each of the dough pieces into a thin oval shape about 10 inches long and 5 inches wide. Make sure the edges are slightly thicker than the center. This helps form the boat shape and keeps the filling from spilling out.

Fold the edges in over themselves—imagine you're making a stuffed-crust pizza, minus the stuffing. This will make a thick, round perimeter for your boat. Now pull and twist the two ends tightly to form the boat—this prevents the dough from unraveling while baking. Transfer as many of the dough boats as will fit to a floured pizza peel (see Tips).

Add enough of the cheese mixture to fill the center of each boat generously without overflowing, then brush the edges with the egg wash. Transfer the khachapuri onto the pizza steel and bake until the dough is lightly golden and the cheese is melted, 6 to 8 minutes.

Using tongs or a pizza peel, remove the khachapuri from the oven. Use the back of a spoon to create a small indentation in the center of each boat, then crack an egg into each indentation. Return the boats to the oven until the egg whites are set but the yolk remains runny, 4 to 6 more minutes.

Remove the boats from the oven, then top each with 1 tablespoon of butter and let it melt into the hot, gooey cheese. Finish with a sprinkle of flaky sea salt and ground black pepper.

To enjoy, use a fork to break the yolk, swirl it into the melted cheese, and rip off a piece of the crust to dip into that cheesy goodness.

MORIBYAN'S TIPS

If you don't have a pizza steel, use an upside-down baking sheet.

If you don't have a pizza peel, simply use a sheet of parchment paper to transfer the khachapuri to the pizza steel or baking tray.

STAUB
STAUB

DUTCH BABY PANCAKE

The Dutch baby is hands-down the easiest, most impressive breakfast you can make. If you've never had one, it's a giant, puffy pancake that's crispy around the edges but almost custard-like in the center. The batter comes together in under five minutes. Just toss everything in a blender, pour it into a hot skillet, and let the oven do the work. You might want to pitch a tent right outside the oven because you won't want to miss the show through the window as it rises high and forms those golden, puffy edges. Finish with powdered sugar, maple syrup, and fresh fruit, and you've got a showstopper.

SERVES 4

- ¾ cup (105g) all-purpose flour
- ¼ cup (50g) granulated sugar
- ¼ teaspoon salt
- 3 large eggs, at room temperature
- 1½ teaspoons vanilla extract
- ¾ cup (180g) whole milk
- 3 tablespoons unsalted butter

FOR SERVING

- Powdered sugar
- Fresh berries
- Maple syrup
- Fresh lemon zest and/or juice (optional)

Preheat the oven to 425°F and place a 10- or 12-inch skillet inside to heat up for about 20 minutes.

Meanwhile, in a blender, combine the flour, granulated sugar, salt, eggs, vanilla, and milk. Blend until smooth, then let the batter rest while the skillet finishes heating. (You can also hand-whisk it in a bowl.)

Carefully take the skillet out of the oven and add the butter. Swirl it around the pan until it's completely melted and coats the bottom and sides. Work quickly to prevent the skillet from cooling down too much.

Pour the batter directly into the center of the pan, slowly and carefully, keeping the stream in one spot the whole time so it spreads evenly on its own.

Immediately return the skillet to the oven and bake until the Dutch baby is puffed up and golden, 12 to 13 minutes. Reduce the heat to 375°F and bake until the center is set, 6 to 7 more minutes.

Serve warm with your favorite toppings like powdered sugar, berries, syrup, or lemon zest/juice.

CINNAMON ROLL PANCAKES

If you're anything like me, you probably don't treat yourself to a proper breakfast at home as often as you should. Enter these cinnamon roll pancakes. They give you everything you love about warm, gooey cinnamon rolls without all the rising, kneading, and patience. You'll whip up a simple pancake batter, swirl in buttery cinnamon-sugar goodness, and let the magic happen. And to take them over the top? A luscious maple cream cheese glaze that melts into every warm, fluffy bite. It's a little more time and effort than your average pancake, but totally worth it for making an ordinary morning special.

MAKES ABOUT 10 PANCAKES

MAPLE CREAM CHEESE GLAZE

- ½ cup powdered sugar, plus more to taste
- 4 ounces cream cheese, at room temperature
- 4 tablespoons (2 ounces/55g) unsalted butter, at room temperature
- ¼ cup maple syrup

BATTER

- 2¼ cups (315g) all-purpose flour
- ¼ cup (50g) granulated sugar
- 1 tablespoon baking powder
- 1 teaspoon baking soda
- ½ teaspoon salt
- 2 large eggs
- 2 cups (460g) buttermilk
- 4 tablespoons (2 ounces/55g) unsalted butter, melted and cooled slightly
- 2 teaspoons vanilla extract

CINNAMON BUTTER

- ½ cup packed light brown sugar, plus more as needed
- 5 tablespoons (2.5 ounces/70g) unsalted butter, melted
- 1 tablespoon ground cinnamon

Make the maple cream cheese glaze: In a stand mixer fitted with the paddle (or in a medium bowl with a hand mixer), beat together the powdered sugar, cream cheese, butter, and maple syrup until smooth and creamy. Set aside.

Make the batter: In a large bowl, whisk together the flour, granulated sugar, baking powder, baking soda, and salt.

In a separate bowl, whisk together the eggs, buttermilk, melted butter, and vanilla until well combined.

Pour the buttermilk mixture into the flour mixture and stir until just combined. Be careful not to overmix.

Make the cinnamon butter: In a small bowl, mix together the brown sugar, butter, and cinnamon just until well combined. Let it cool down until just slightly thickened, 10 to 15 minutes; you're looking for a paste that has a nut-butter consistency. Transfer to a piping bag or a plastic sandwich bag (once filled, cut off the corner of the sandwich bag to make a piping "tip").

Preheat a large nonstick skillet over medium heat.

Working in batches, pour about ¼ cup of pancake batter per pancake onto the preheated pan. After about 1 minute of cooking, pipe the cinnamon butter in a circular motion on top of the pancake in the shape of a spiral.

Continue to cook the pancake until the bottom is golden brown and the cinnamon butter has begun to caramelize, 1 to 2 minutes.

Flip the pancake over and cook the other side until golden brown and fully cooked through, 1 to 2 minutes. Transfer to a plate and cover with a clean towel while you cook the remaining pancakes. (Alternatively, you can keep them warm on a baking sheet in a 200°F oven, loosely covered with foil.)

Once the pancakes are done, warm up the glaze in the microwave for 15 seconds if needed. Spread over each pancake to enjoy!

BROWN BUTTER BELGIAN WAFFLES

Growing up, the best part of any vacation was when my parents booked a hotel with a full breakfast bar. My brothers and I would rush downstairs every morning, racing to see if they had a DIY waffle maker. We'd compete to make the crispiest, most golden waffles, pretending to be chefs. Waffles will always have a special place in my heart, and honestly, I'll choose them over pancakes or French toast any day. This recipe takes it up a notch with brown butter, giving the waffles a rich, nutty flavor. A little trick: Sprinkle sugar on the waffle maker before cooking for a perfectly crispy texture.

MAKES ABOUT SIX 7-INCH WAFFLES

- 8 tablespoons (4 ounces/115g) unsalted butter, plus 2 to 3 tablespoons for coating the waffle iron
- 1¾ cups (245g) all-purpose flour
- ⅓ cup (65g) sugar, plus ¼ cup (50g) for coating the waffle iron
- ¼ cup (30g) cornstarch
- 1 tablespoon baking powder
- ½ teaspoon baking soda
- ¾ teaspoon salt
- 1¾ cups (405g) buttermilk
- 1 teaspoon vanilla extract
- 3 large eggs, separated

FOR SERVING

- Whipped cream
- Fresh fruit
- Maple syrup

Heat a waffle iron to medium-high to high while you make the batter.

In a small saucepan, melt the 8 tablespoons unsalted butter over medium heat. Once completely melted, stir constantly as it begins to foam. Continue cooking until the butter turns golden brown and tiny brown specks form at the bottom, 8 to 11 minutes. Once it smells nutty and reaches a deep golden brown, immediately remove it from the heat. Let it cool until warm to the touch before using.

In a large bowl, whisk together the flour, ⅓ cup of the sugar, the cornstarch, baking powder, baking soda, and salt.

In another bowl, whisk together the buttermilk, brown butter, vanilla, and egg yolks until smooth.

Gradually add the buttermilk mixture to the flour mixture, stirring until just combined. Be careful not to overmix.

In a clean bowl, with an electric mixer, beat the egg whites on medium-high speed until stiff peaks form, 3 to 5 minutes. Gently fold the whipped egg whites into the batter, being careful not to deflate the mixture.

Butter the bottom of the waffle iron with the remaining 2 to 3 tablespoons butter. Sprinkle a little bit of sugar all across, about 1 teaspoon. Pour 1 cup of batter into the preheated waffle iron, spreading it evenly. Sprinkle more sugar on top of the batter and grease the top of the waffle iron. Seal it shut tightly and cook until the waffles are golden brown and crispy, 4 to 6 minutes.

Serve hot with your favorite toppings, such as whipped cream, fruit, and syrup.

MORIBYAN'S TIP

Place the waffles on a wire rack in a 200°F oven to keep them warm and crispy while you repeat with the remaining waffles.

CRISPY TATER TOT EGG CUPS

Here's a fun, easy breakfast idea: loaded Tater Tot egg cups. Picture crispy, golden Tater Tots pressed into a muffin tin to form a crunchy base. Then, layer in some melty cheese and savory breakfast sausage before cracking a fresh egg right on top. Pop it in the oven, and you'll have a hot, satisfying breakfast that's crispy on the outside but protein-packed, cheesy, and eggy on the inside. It's like having your whole breakfast in one little cup, perfect for busy mornings or when you need something easy to grab and go!

MAKES 12 CUPS TO SERVE 6

- Avocado oil cooking spray
- 2-pound bag frozen Tater Tots (about 60), thawed
- ½ cup finely shredded cheddar cheese
- ½ cup crumbled or chopped cooked turkey sausage
- 12 medium eggs (see Tip)
- ½ teaspoon sea salt, or to taste
- ¼ teaspoon freshly ground black pepper, or to taste

Preheat the oven to 400°F. Spray 12 cups of a standard muffin tin with avocado oil.

Divide the Tater Tots among the muffin cups, about 5 tots per cup, and mash them down completely, pressing them up the sides to form a cup shape that goes all the way to the top of the tin.

Sprinkle 1 tablespoon cheddar into each Tater Tot cup and transfer to the oven.

Bake until deeply golden brown and crispy, 17 to 18 minutes.

Remove from the oven, add a few pieces of crumbled turkey sausage on top of the cheese, then carefully crack an egg into each cup and sprinkle with sea salt and black pepper.

Bake until the whites are set but the yolks are still slightly runny or to your preferred doneness, 9 to 10 minutes.

Gently remove from the tin and allow to cool for 5 minutes on a wire rack, then enjoy!

MORIBYAN'S TIP

Most recipes call for large eggs and you can absolutely use them here. If you can find medium eggs, though, they are a better fit since some large eggs can spill over the sides of the Tater Tot cups once cracked in. Either size works and both will taste great, just keep in mind that medium makes for a tidier fit.

PHILLY CHEESESTEAK EGGS BENEDICT

I lived in Philadelphia for two years, so it's no surprise I'm always finding new ways to turn a Philly cheesesteak into just about anything! The dish is rich, hearty, and definitely not the lightest in the book, but that's exactly why I love it.

MAKES 8 BENEDICTS TO SERVE 4

PEPPER AND ONION

1 tablespoon olive oil

1 green bell pepper, thinly sliced

½ yellow onion, roughly chopped

2 teaspoons minced garlic

STEAK

1 tablespoon unsalted butter

1½ teaspoons neutral oil

1 pound thinly shaved rib-eye steak

1 teaspoon paprika

¾ teaspoon salt

½ teaspoon mustard powder

¼ teaspoon freshly ground black pepper

2 tablespoons Worcestershire sauce

¼ cup beef broth

4 slices white American cheese

HOLLANDAISE SAUCE

4 egg yolks

2 teaspoons fresh lemon juice

1 teaspoon yellow mustard

Pinch of cayenne pepper

¼ teaspoon salt

6 tablespoons (85g/¾ stick) unsalted butter, melted and hot (but not browned)

ASSEMBLY

1 tablespoon distilled white vinegar

8 large eggs

4 English muffins, homemade (see page 208) or store-bought, split open and toasted

Chopped chives, for garnish

Cook the pepper and onion: In a large sauté pan, heat the oil over medium heat. Add the bell pepper, onions, and garlic and sauté until soft and fragrant, 8 to 10 minutes. Transfer to a plate and set aside.

Cook the steak: In the same pan, heat the butter and neutral oil over medium-high heat. Add the shaved steak and season with the paprika, salt, mustard powder, and black pepper. Cook until deeply browned, 6 to 8 minutes.

Pour in the Worcestershire sauce and beef broth and simmer until the liquid reduces and the steak is tender, about 2 minutes. Stir the pepper and onion into the steak mixture. Add the cheese and mix until combined.

Make the hollandaise sauce: Using an immersion blender (see Tip), in a tall jar or cup, combine the egg yolks, lemon juice, mustard, cayenne, and salt. Start blending and, with the motor running, slowly drizzle in the hot butter and blend until the sauce is smooth. Keep warm until ready to serve.

Assemble the eggs Benedict: Bring a pot of water to a gentle simmer and add the distilled vinegar.

Crack an egg into a small bowl or ramekin. Swirl the water with a spoon and carefully drop the egg into the center. Repeat with a second egg, dropping it away from the first. Poach the eggs until the whites are set but the yolks remain runny, 3 to 4 minutes. Remove with a slotted spoon and drain on a paper towel, then repeat with the remaining eggs.

Place 2 halves of a toasted English muffin on each of four plates. Spoon the cheesy Philly cheesesteak mixture on top of each muffin half. Gently place a poached egg on each muffin half, then drizzle with hollandaise sauce. Garnish with chopped chives and serve immediately.

MORIBYAN'S TIP

If you don't have an immersion blender, make the hollandaise in a double boiler. Place a heatproof bowl over a pot of simmering water, ensuring the bottom of the bowl doesn't touch the water. In the bowl, whisk together egg yolks, lemon juice, and mustard until slightly thickened. Slowly drizzle in warm melted butter while whisking continuously to create a smooth, creamy emulsion. Keep whisking until the sauce thickens to a silky consistency. Season with salt and a pinch of cayenne.

ARAB FUSION BREAKFAST BURRITOS

My mom is famous for her breakfasts. On weekends, we would wake up to the smell of eggs sizzling in the pan, warm pita, and ful medames simmering on the stove. She would lay out a full spread, from cured meats like basturma to Arab cheese, crispy homemade potatoes, and a Libyan salad called sharmoula. So, I thought why not take all that goodness and wrap it up into one warm handheld burrito packed with sujuk (a Turkish sausage) and fried Halloumi? I know mom would approve.

SERVES 4

CILANTRO JALAPEÑO SAUCE

- A generous handful (about 1 cup) cilantro leaves and tender stems
- 2 jalapeños, halved (seeded if you prefer less heat)
- 2 garlic cloves, left whole
- ½ cup mayonnaise
- ⅓ cup whole-milk plain yogurt
- Juice of 1 lime, plus more to taste
- ½ teaspoon smoked paprika
- ¼ teaspoon salt, plus more to taste
- ¼ teaspoon freshly ground black pepper

FUL MEDAMES

- 2 tablespoons extra-virgin olive oil
- 2 teaspoons minced garlic
- 2 green onions, thinly sliced
- 1 (16-ounce) can fava beans, drained and rinsed
- 1 teaspoon ground cumin
- 1 teaspoon sweet paprika
- 1 teaspoon dried parsley
- ¼ teaspoon salt
- 2 tablespoons finely chopped fresh cilantro
- 1 tablespoon fresh lemon juice

BURRITOS

- Neutral oil
- 8 ounces sujuk (Turkish sausage), cut into small pieces
- 8 large eggs, whisked
- Salt and freshly ground black pepper
- 6 ounces Halloumi cheese, sliced into thin strips or cubes
- 4 burrito-size (9-inch) flour tortillas, homemade (see page 211) or store-bought

Make the cilantro jalapeño sauce: In a blender or food processor, combine all the ingredients and blend until completely smooth and creamy. Taste and adjust salt or lime as needed. Refrigerate until ready to use.

Make the ful medames: In a saucepan, heat the olive oil over medium heat. Add the garlic and sauté until fragrant, about 30 seconds. Toss in the green onions and cook for another minute until just softened.

Add the fava beans, ½ cup water, the cumin, sweet paprika, dried parsley, and salt. Reduce the heat to low and let it simmer together for about 20 minutes, gently mashing some but not all the beans with the back of your spoon to create a chunky, creamy texture. Turn off the heat, stir in the cilantro and lemon juice, and set aside.

For the burritos: In a large sauté pan, heat some neutral oil over medium heat. Add the sujuk pieces and cook until browned and fragrant, 3 to 5 minutes. Transfer to a bowl and set aside.

Season the eggs with salt and pepper. Heat the pan you used for the sujuk (use a little more oil, if needed) over medium heat. Pour in the eggs and cook gently, stirring slowly with a spatula, until soft scrambled and just set. Remove from the heat and keep warm.

Clean the pan, then heat it over medium-high, add a drizzle of oil, and sear the Halloumi until golden brown, 1 to 2 minutes per side. Set aside.

Warm the flour tortillas so they're pliable, either in the microwave for 30 seconds or briefly over the stove.

On each tortilla, layer a scoop of ful medames, some scrambled eggs, a scoop of sujuk, a few pieces of Halloumi, and a drizzle of cilantro jalapeño sauce. Fold in the sides and roll tightly into a burrito.

Brush a skillet with neutral oil over medium heat. Place as many of the burritos as will fit seam-side down and toast until all sides are golden and crisp, 2 to 3 minutes per side. Repeat with the remaining burritos if needed.

Cut in half, serve with extra sauce on the side, and enjoy!

PARATHA BREAKFAST ROLLS

When my husband and I visited Dubai, my cousin, who's a local, took us to her favorite brunch spot and one of the first things to hit the table was an egg and paratha roll-up. From the first bite, I was hooked. When we continued our trip to Oman, I searched for it everywhere and ended up having it every single morning. It's just flaky, buttery paratha wrapped around soft, fluffy eggs, but somehow, it's perfection. At the cafés, it always came with creamy spreadable cheese like Kiri, which is super popular across Arab countries, but you can use whatever cheese you love. You can easily find frozen paratha in most grocery stores to make this an easy ten-minute recipe or make it from scratch (see page 216). I like to roll it up and slice it into little bites.

MAKES 2 ROLLS

- 4 large eggs
- Salt and freshly ground black pepper
- Neutral oil or ghee
- 2 frozen parathas, cooked according to package instructions
- Cheddar slices or spreadable cheese, such as Kiri

Crack the eggs into a bowl or mixing cup and season with salt and black pepper. Whisk well to combine.

Heat a nonstick skillet, about the same size as the paratha, over medium heat and coat it with oil or ghee.

Pour half of the egg mixture into the pan to cover the entire surface and cook undisturbed until the bottom is set but the top still looks glossy and wet, 2 to 3 minutes.

Place a cooked paratha on top of the eggs and press gently so it sticks. Continue cooking until the eggs are fully set, 2 more minutes.

Flip the paratha and egg onto a plate so the egg side is exposed.

Add your cheese of choice—either cheddar slices for a melty bite or spreadable Kiri cheese for a creamy texture. Starting from one edge, roll up the paratha tightly, then repeat with the remaining egg and paratha.

Using a serrated knife, slice each roll into 2- to 3-inch pieces to enjoy!

BEEF CHORIZO

Chorizo is usually made from pork, so I never get to order it when I'm eating out. It's also hard to find a good version in grocery stores. That's why I wanted to make it from scratch so we can all enjoy those spicy, savory flavors anytime the craving hits. It's delicious in breakfast tacos, breakfast burritos, or even in a pasta dish like the chorizo and chicken recipe on my blog.

MAKES 1 POUND

SPICE BLEND

- 1 tablespoon ancho chile powder
- 1½ teaspoons sweet paprika
- 1 teaspoon smoked paprika
- 1 teaspoon ground cumin
- 1 teaspoon ground coriander
- 1 teaspoon onion powder
- 1½ teaspoons salt, or to taste
- ½ teaspoon freshly ground black pepper
- ¼ teaspoon cayenne pepper, or more if you like heat

CHILE PASTE AND BEEF

- 3 dried guajillo chiles
- ¼ cup apple cider vinegar
- 1 tablespoon minced garlic
- 1 teaspoon dried oregano
- ½ teaspoon dried thyme
- 1 pound ground beef (80/20)

Make the spice blend: In a small bowl, combine the ancho powder, sweet paprika, smoked paprika, cumin, coriander, onion powder, salt, black pepper, and cayenne. Set aside.

Make the chile paste: Remove the stems and seeds from the guajillos and place them in a heatproof bowl. Pour just enough hot water to cover and let them soak until softened, about 10 minutes.

Reserving the soaking water, drain the chiles and transfer to a mini food processor or blender. Add the vinegar, garlic, oregano, and thyme. Blend until smooth. If it's still too chunky, drizzle in a little of the soaking water (or plain water) to help it break down. Keep going until you get a smooth, pourable consistency.

Season the beef: Pour the chile paste and spice blend over the beef, then use clean hands to mix everything thoroughly.

Divide the meat into 2 equal portions. Roll each into a log using plastic wrap, then wrap tightly to seal the ends. It should resemble a large sausage log. Refrigerate for a few hours or overnight to let the flavors develop and the texture firm up. Store in the fridge for up to 5 days, or in the freezer in freezer-safe bags for up to 2 months.

MORIBYAN'S TIP

To use this for breakfast tacos, cook the beef chorizo in a skillet over medium heat, breaking it up as it browns, until fully cooked. Warm flour tortillas (either in the microwave or in a dry skillet, just so they don't tear) and fill with any combo of chorizo, scrambled or fried eggs, smashed avocado or guacamole, crispy potatoes or Tater Tots, salsa, and chopped cilantro.

TEASPOON

KIMCHI AND GOCHUJANG SHAKSHUKA

My mom had a tradition of making shakshuka every Saturday for breakfast, and it was one of the first dishes I learned to make. While shakshuka is distinctly North African, I later realized many other cultures have their own versions of eggs simmered in spiced tomato sauce, like Italy's eggs in purgatory or Turkey's menemen. Growing up in Southern California, I was surrounded by incredible Korean food, and one of my favorite dishes to order was tteokbokki, chewy rice cakes simmered in a spicy red sauce. When I finally visited Seoul, I noticed how many Korean dishes revolved around bold red sauces, just like the North African ones I grew up with. That connection sparked the idea to bring the two together, and when I added kimchi and gochujang to my mom's shakshuka, it felt almost like they were always meant to be together.

SERVES 4

- 2 tablespoons neutral oil
- 1 teaspoon toasted sesame oil
- 3 tablespoons gochujang, plus more to taste
- 1 tablespoon tomato paste
- 3 Roma tomatoes, diced
- 1 tablespoon minced garlic
- ½ cup chopped kimchi
- 1 tablespoon soy sauce
- 1 tablespoon sugar
- ¼ teaspoon salt, or to taste
- 4 or 5 large eggs

FOR SERVING

- Chopped green onions, for garnish
- Gochugaru or red chile flakes (optional), for garnish
- Toasted sesame seeds (optional), for garnish
- Bread, such as pita or sourdough, or steamed rice

In a large skillet, heat the neutral and sesame oils over medium heat. Add the gochujang and tomato paste and cook, stirring, until the color deepens, 1 to 2 minutes.

Add the diced tomatoes and garlic and cook, stirring occasionally, until softened, about 4 minutes. Once softened, break down the tomatoes a bit by mashing with a wooden spoon.

Stir in the kimchi, soy sauce, and sugar. Cook for 2 to 3 more minutes to let the flavors meld.

Add ⅓ cup water (or ½ cup if you prefer a thin sauce) and the salt. Stir well to combine. Simmer until the sauce thickens slightly, 8 to 10 minutes.

Use the back of a spoon to make small wells in the sauce and crack an egg into each well. Cover the skillet with a lid, reduce the heat to low, and cook until the eggs are set to your liking, 5 to 7 minutes.

To serve: Garnish with green onions. If desired, also top with gochugaru and toasted sesame seeds. Serve immediately with bread or steamed rice.

JAPANESE-INSPIRED EGG SANDOS

You might be thinking, "It's just an egg salad sandwich," but trust me, this one is special. When I visited Japan, I basically lived off these egg sandos from the *konbini,* or Japanese convenience stores. And if you've ever been to a konbini, you know those aren't your average gas station snacks. These sandwiches are soft, creamy, perfectly seasoned, and taste like comfort in every bite. The secret is umami-packed Japanese mayo and the fluffiest milk bread that practically melts in your mouth. I like to keep mine simple, just like the ones I grabbed daily in Tokyo, but you can dress it up with a little chili oil, green onions, or thinly sliced cucumber if you're feeling extra.

SERVES 4

EGG SALAD

- 6 large eggs
- ¼ cup Kewpie mayonnaise
- 1 teaspoon yellow mustard
- ½ teaspoon sugar
- ¼ to ½ teaspoon salt, to taste
- ¼ teaspoon freshly ground black pepper, or to taste
- 2 to 3 tablespoons heavy cream or milk
- 2 green onions (optional), green parts only, thinly sliced

ASSEMBLY

- 8 slices (½- to ¾-inch-thick) Japanese milk bread or any sliced soft white bread
- Salted butter, at room temperature
- Thinly sliced cucumber (optional)

Set up a bowl of ice and water and have near the stove. Bring a small pot of water to a boil. Reduce to a gentle simmer, then carefully lower the eggs (in the shell) into the pot. Cook the eggs so the yolk is mostly set but still slightly soft, for 8 to 9 minutes. Transfer the eggs immediately to the ice bath. Let it sit for 5 minutes or until cool enough to handle.

Crack and peel the eggs. Separate the egg yolks from the egg whites. Place the egg yolks in a bowl and the egg whites on a cutting board. Dice the egg whites into small pieces. Set aside.

To the bowl with the egg yolks, add the Kewpie mayo, mustard, sugar, salt, black pepper, and 2 tablespoons cream or milk. Mash the yolks and mix it all together, adding more cream or milk as needed for a thick sauce or paste consistency.

Add the chopped egg whites to the bowl and chopped green onions (if using) and fold to combine, taking care not to break the egg whites.

Assemble the sandos: Slice the crusts off the bread and spread butter on one side of each slice. Add thinly sliced cucumber to one side, if desired, and then egg filling on top. Seal the sandwich shut with the other piece of bread and cut in half to enjoy! Wrap them up tight and they'll keep for up to 3 days in the fridge.

BAKED FETA EGG CASSEROLE

By the time this book comes out, people might not even remember that viral baked feta and tomato pasta from TikTok. You know the one that had everyone rushing to grab feta, causing it to sell out for weeks. I loved the dish and never quite got over it, even after the trend fizzled out. Feta on its own can be a bit strong, but when you roast it with tomatoes, it caramelizes and becomes a creamy, flavorful base. Instead of adding pasta, we're baking eggs right into the mix, creating a Mediterranean-inspired dish that's perfect for breakfast.

SERVES 2 TO 4

¼ cup olive oil
1 teaspoon dried oregano
Salt and freshly ground black pepper
½ teaspoon red pepper flakes
1 (8-ounce) block feta cheese
2 cups cherry tomatoes
1 red bell pepper, diced
½ cup whole-milk ricotta cheese
3 large basil leaves, chopped
1 tablespoon finely chopped fresh parsley
2 teaspoons finely minced garlic
4 large eggs
Toasty bread, for serving

Preheat the oven to 400°F.

In a small bowl, whisk together the olive oil, oregano, ½ teaspoon salt, ½ teaspoon black pepper, and the pepper flakes.

Place the block of feta cheese right in the center of an 8 × 8-inch square pan. Surround it with the cherry tomatoes and chopped red bell pepper. Drizzle the seasoned olive oil evenly over the feta and all the veggies.

Bake until the tomatoes are blistered and juicy and the feta is golden and soft, 25 minutes.

Remove the pan from the oven and reduce the oven temperature to 350°F.

Stir the tomatoes and peppers with the melted feta to create a creamy, flavorful base. Then add the ricotta, chopped basil, parsley, and garlic and mix until everything is combined.

Use a spoon to make four wells in the mixture and crack an egg into each one. Sprinkle the eggs with a little salt and black pepper.

Pop it back into the oven and bake until the egg whites are set but the yolks are still a little runny or jammy, 8 to 10 minutes. Keep in mind the eggs will continue to cook slightly from the residual heat as they rest.

Serve hot with toasty bread on the side.

SALADS, SMALL BITES & SIDES

MOROCCAN-INSPIRED CARROT SALAD

with Couscous

I wanted to find a way to make salads extra exciting, like the kind you actually crave and can't put your fork down when eating. This one is inspired by a classic Moroccan carrot salad, but I gave it a twist to make it heartier. I swap the usual boiled carrot rounds for shredded raw carrots to keep that fresh crunch, then add couscous for a nice chew and raisins for a touch of sweetness. And the dressing? It's a dreamy mix of tahini, harissa, and honey to give you the perfect balance of sweet, nutty, and tangy spice.

SERVES 4 TO 6

PEARL COUSCOUS

- ½ teaspoon salt
- 1½ teaspoons olive oil
- 1 cup pearl couscous

DRESSING

- ¼ cup olive oil
- 2 tablespoons harissa paste
- 2 tablespoons fresh lemon juice
- 1 tablespoon honey
- 1 tablespoon tahini
- 1 teaspoon finely minced garlic
- ½ teaspoon salt, or more to taste
- ½ teaspoon freshly ground black pepper
- ½ teaspoon ground cumin
- Pinch of cayenne pepper or red pepper flakes (optional, for heat)

ASSEMBLY

- ¼ cup raisins
- 12 ounces carrots (6 large or 9 small), grated on the large holes of a box grater
- 2 tablespoons finely chopped fresh cilantro
- 2 green onions, thinly sliced
- 4 fresh mint leaves, chopped

Cook the pearl couscous: In a saucepan, bring 1 cup water, the salt, and olive oil to a boil. Stir in the pearl couscous, reduce the heat, cover, and let cook for about 10 minutes. Turn off the heat and let it steam, still covered, for another 10 minutes. Fluff the couscous with a fork, then transfer it to a tray to cool down faster.

Meanwhile, make the dressing: In a small bowl, whisk together the olive oil, harissa, lemon juice, honey, tahini, garlic, salt, black pepper, cumin, and the cayenne or pepper flakes (if you want extra heat). Mix until smooth and creamy.

Assemble the salad: Place the raisins in a small heatproof bowl and cover them with hot water. Let them soak until they become plump and soft, 5 to 10 minutes. Drain and set aside.

In a large bowl, combine the cooled couscous, grated carrots, cilantro, soaked and drained raisins, green onions, and mint leaves. Pour as much dressing as you'd like over the mixture. I recommend starting with two-thirds, then add more to taste and toss everything well to coat evenly. Serve immediately or cover and refrigerate to enjoy later!

MEDITERRANEAN SALAD

with Farro & Date Vinaigrette

Let's be real, sometimes salads need a little something extra to make them feel like a full meal. This one is packed with sweet potatoes, which are the perfect match for the sweet and earthy date vinaigrette. Farro adds chew, texture, and a boost of fiber, making it even more satisfying. Kale is usually a hard sell in our house, but my husband and I went back for seconds and thirds. And if you want to take it up another notch, toss in some roasted nuts for a little crunch.

SERVES 4

SWEET POTATO

- 12 ounces sweet potato (about 1 medium), peeled and cut into ¾-inch cubes
- 1 tablespoon neutral oil
- ½ teaspoon salt
- ¼ teaspoon freshly ground black pepper

FARRO

- ¾ cup pearled farro
- 1 tablespoon unsalted butter
- ½ teaspoon salt

DATE VINAIGRETTE

- ¼ cup neutral oil
- 3 tablespoons white balsamic vinegar
- 4 Medjool dates, pitted and soaked in hot water for 5 minutes
- 1½ teaspoons yellow mustard
- 1 teaspoon finely minced garlic
- ½ teaspoon salt
- ½ teaspoon freshly ground black pepper

ASSEMBLY

- 5 cups chopped kale
- ½ cup crumbled feta cheese
- ¼ large red onion, thinly sliced
- 1 teaspoon ground sumac

Roast the sweet potato: Preheat the oven to 425°F.

In a bowl, toss the cubed sweet potato with the neutral oil, salt, and black pepper. Spread the cubes in a single layer on a baking sheet.

Roast for 30 minutes, shaking or flipping them every 10 minutes, until tender and lightly caramelized. Set aside to cool.

Cook the farro: Rinse the pearled farro under cold water in a fine-mesh sieve.

In a medium saucepan, melt the butter over medium heat. Add the pearled farro and toast it, stirring frequently, until fragrant and lightly golden, 2 to 3 minutes.

Add 1¼ cups water and the salt and bring to a boil. Reduce the heat, cover, and cook until all the water is absorbed and the farro is tender, 25 to 30 minutes. Remove from heat and let it sit, covered, for a few minutes. Then transfer the farro to a plate and spread it all around to cool faster.

Make the date vinaigrette: In a blender or food processor, combine the neutral oil, vinegar, dates, mustard, garlic, salt, pepper, and 3 tablespoons water. Blend until smooth and creamy. If you prefer a thinner dressing, add an extra tablespoon of water. Set aside.

Assemble the salad: Massage the chopped kale with about two-thirds of the date vinaigrette until the kale becomes tender. Add the cooled sweet potato cubes, farro, crumbled feta, red onion slices, and sumac. Drizzle the remaining vinaigrette, or as much as you like, over the salad and toss gently to combine.

FATTOUSH

There wasn't a day when my mom didn't whip up a salad for the dinner table. Sometimes it was a Libyan salad called sharmoula, and other times it was fattoush with little twists depending on what she had in the fridge. What really makes this classic Levant salad shine are two things: the tangy, slight sweetness from pomegranate molasses in the dressing, and pita fried fresh and tossed in at the last minute so it stays perfectly crispy. And don't forget the fresh mint. It keeps the salad cool and refreshing. Fattoush has always been my favorite, and it's the one I now make all the time in my own kitchen. A lot of traditional recipes also use green onions and radishes, but I love swapping them out for pepperoncini and olives, so feel free to tweak it to your taste.

SERVES 4 TO 6

POMEGRANATE DRESSING

- ¼ cup olive oil
- 1 tablespoon pomegranate molasses
- 2 tablespoons fresh lemon juice
- 1 teaspoon minced garlic
- 1 teaspoon ground sumac
- ½ teaspoon salt, or to taste
- ½ teaspoon dried mint
- ¼ teaspoon freshly ground black pepper
- ⅛ teaspoon ground allspice

CRISPY PITA

- Vegetable oil, for shallow-frying
- 2 pita breads, torn into bite-size pieces
- Salt and freshly ground black pepper

SALAD

- 1 large head romaine lettuce, chopped thin
- 1 cup diced Persian (mini) cucumbers (from 1 medium or 2 small)
- 2 Roma tomatoes, diced
- ¼ cup chopped fresh mint leaves
- ¼ cup finely chopped fresh parsley
- Optional add-ins: pitted olives, chopped pepperoncini, thinly sliced radishes, or green onions

Make the pomegranate dressing: In a small jar or bowl, combine the olive oil, pomegranate molasses, lemon juice, garlic, sumac, salt, dried mint, black pepper, and allspice. Seal the jar and shake well until fully emulsified or whisk in a bowl until smooth. Set aside while you prepare the rest of the salad.

Make the crispy pita: Line a plate with paper towels and have near the stove. Pour ½ inch of vegetable oil into a medium skillet and heat over medium heat until shimmering. To test if the oil is ready, drop in one piece of pita. It should sizzle and begin to bubble immediately.

Working in batches to avoid overcrowding, add the rest of the pita pieces and fry, stirring occasionally, until the pita is golden and crisp on all sides, 2 to 4 minutes per batch. Transfer to the paper towels to drain. While still warm, sprinkle lightly with salt and black pepper. Let cool completely.

Assemble the salad: In a large bowl, combine the chopped romaine, cucumbers, tomatoes, fresh mint, parsley, and any optional add-ins. Drizzle the dressing over the top and toss well until everything is evenly coated. Taste and adjust the seasoning as needed.

Just before serving, add the fried pita chips on top for that irresistible crunch. Serve fresh and enjoy immediately!

CHICKEN CAESAR PASTA SALAD

We all know Caesar salad is the best salad . . . but now let's make it even better by adding pasta! You still get the crisp lettuce, crunchy croutons, juicy chicken, and creamy dressing, but the pasta makes it heartier and even more satisfying. It's the perfect cold, refreshing meal you'll crave during the hot summer months.

SERVES 6 TO 8

CHICKEN

- 2 tablespoons olive oil, plus more for the pan
- 2 teaspoons Italian seasoning
- ¾ teaspoon salt
- 1 teaspoon garlic powder
- ½ teaspoon freshly ground black pepper
- ½ teaspoon red pepper flakes
- 2 boneless, skinless chicken breasts (about 1 pound)

DRESSING

- 1 cup mayonnaise
- ½ cup freshly grated Parmesan cheese
- ¼ cup buttermilk
- 1 tablespoon fresh lemon juice
- 1½ teaspoons Worcestershire sauce
- 1½ teaspoons minced fresh garlic
- 2 teaspoons yellow mustard
- ½ to 1 teaspoon anchovy paste, to taste
- ½ teaspoon freshly ground black pepper

ASSEMBLY

- 12 ounces penne pasta
- 2 heads romaine lettuce, chopped
- 1 to 2 tablespoons finely chopped fresh parsley
- 1 cup crushed croutons

Cook the chicken: In a medium bowl, mix together the olive oil, Italian seasoning, salt, garlic powder, black pepper, and pepper flakes. Add the chicken breasts and turn to coat evenly.

In a skillet, heat a light drizzle of olive oil over medium heat. Add the chicken and cook until golden on both sides and fully cooked, 5 to 6 minutes per side. Let rest for 10 minutes, then slice into bite-size pieces. Transfer to a large bowl, cover, and refrigerate until chilled.

Make the dressing: In a bowl, whisk together the mayonnaise, Parmesan, buttermilk, lemon juice, Worcestershire sauce, minced garlic, mustard, anchovy paste, and black pepper. Mix until smooth.

To assemble: In a pot of boiling water, cook the pasta according to the package directions. Drain, rinse, and let cool.

When the chicken is chilled, add the cooled pasta, romaine, parsley, and dressing and toss until evenly coated.

Right before serving, fold in the croutons and toss to combine!

MORIBYAN'S TIP

If you plan to make this a few hours in advance, wait to add the romaine and dressing until right before serving.

ZAALOUK
(Moroccan Roasted Eggplant Dip)

This Moroccan eggplant dip was always on rotation growing up. My mom would make a big batch, and we'd eat it with rice alongside grilled meats at a BBQ. I'd help her in the kitchen to make it sometimes before dinner, mashing down the eggplant as it simmered. Think of it like baba ghanoush but served hot and made without yogurt or tahini. The rich color comes from tomatoes and warm spices that cook down with the eggplant into something smoky and full of flavor. You can fry or roast the eggplant. Roasting is easier and just as delicious, so that's what we're doing here.

SERVES 6 TO 8

- 2 medium globe eggplants (about 2 pounds)
- Salt
- 3 Roma tomatoes
- 4 tablespoons olive oil
- 1 tablespoon tomato paste
- 2 teaspoons minced garlic
- 1½ teaspoons smoked paprika
- 1 teaspoon ground cumin
- ½ teaspoon freshly ground black pepper
- ½ teaspoon ground ginger
- ¼ teaspoon cayenne pepper (optional)
- 2 tablespoons chopped fresh parsley
- 2 tablespoons chopped fresh cilantro
- 1 teaspoon distilled white vinegar or lemon juice

Slice the tops off the eggplants, cut them in half lengthwise, and score the flesh in a crosshatch pattern. Sprinkle the cut sides with ¼ teaspoon salt and place them flesh-side down on a wire rack set over a baking sheet or tray. Let them drain for 30 minutes to draw out excess moisture and any bitterness.

Preheat the oven to 425°F. Line a baking sheet with parchment paper.

Arrange the eggplants, flesh-side down, and the whole Roma tomatoes on the prepared baking sheet. Drizzle with 2 tablespoons of the olive oil and roast until tender and slightly charred, 30 to 40 minutes.

Once cool enough to handle, scoop out the eggplant flesh and roughly chop it. Peel the tomatoes and finely chop or mash the flesh.

In a skillet, heat 1 tablespoon of the olive oil over medium heat. Add the tomato paste and garlic and sauté for a minute until fragrant and deepened in color. Stir in the chopped eggplant and tomatoes, then add ½ to ¾ teaspoon salt (to taste), the smoked paprika, cumin, black pepper, ginger, and cayenne (if using). Let the mixture simmer, stirring often, until thick and almost spreadable, 6 to 7 minutes.

Turn off the heat and fold in the parsley, cilantro, and vinegar. Taste and adjust the seasoning if needed.

Drizzle with the remaining 1 tablespoon olive oil before serving. Enjoy warm. Store in the fridge for up to 1 week.

CHEESY ROASTED GARLIC BREAD

There's already a garlic bread recipe on my blog that everyone loves, but this version is extra special. Roasting the garlic brings out a deep, rich sweetness that is absolutely worth the effort, if you ask me. It takes a bit more time, but it's mostly hands-off. You just wrap a whole head of garlic in foil and let the oven do the work until the cloves are golden and jammy. Once it's mixed into the butter and baked with cheese, you get the most flavorful, melt-in-your-mouth garlic bread. Serve it alongside any pasta recipe in the cookbook and save any leftover roasted garlic butter to slather on steak, chicken, or salmon.

SERVES 8

- 2 large heads garlic
- 1 tablespoon olive oil
- Salt
- 16 tablespoons (227g/2 sticks) unsalted butter, at room temperature
- ⅓ cup grated Parmesan cheese
- ¼ cup finely chopped fresh parsley
- 1 teaspoon dried oregano
- ½ teaspoon freshly ground black pepper
- 1 (16-ounce) loaf French bread
- 1 (8-ounce) block low-moisture mozzarella, shredded on the large holes of a box grater

Preheat the oven to 400°F.

Slice the top off the garlic heads to expose the cloves but leave the cloves otherwise unpeeled. Drizzle with the olive oil, sprinkle with a pinch of salt, wrap in foil, and place on a baking sheet.

Roast until the cloves are golden and soft, 50 to 60 minutes. Remove from the oven but leave the oven on, and reduce the temperature to 350°F.

When the garlic is cool enough to handle, remove and discard the loose outer layers of skin. Squeeze the garlic heads so the roasted garlic cloves pop out into a small bowl. Mash the garlic into a paste with a spoon or fork.

In a bowl, mix the butter with 3 tablespoons of the roasted garlic paste (reserve any additional for another use), the Parmesan, parsley, oregano, ¾ teaspoon salt, and the pepper. Stir until well combined.

Slice the French bread loaf horizontally in half. Place on a baking sheet and spread the garlic butter mixture evenly over both halves so it's fully covered. If you have any extra garlic butter, just store it in an airtight container in the fridge. Sprinkle the mozzarella evenly over both halves.

Bake for 10 minutes, then broil until the cheese is golden and bubbling, 1 to 2 minutes more. Keep a close eye on the bread while it broils. It can go from perfect to burned fast!

Slice and serve warm.

MORIBYAN'S TIP

This makes enough for a large loaf of French bread, but you can easily halve the recipe to serve 4.

FALAFEL

Falafel is way more common in Egypt and the Levant than in North Africa. Even so, every Eid, my family would go all out with a full Arab breakfast spread, and falafel always had a place on the table.

This version is inspired by Egyptian-style falafel, with fava beans instead of chickpeas. For light and fluffy falafel, make sure not to overblend. Once they're fried to golden perfection, tuck them into a pita (see page 227) with tons of veggies, throw them on a salad, or just snack on them with some dip. And while traditional falafel is unstuffed, I once had life-changing cheese-stuffed falafel at a restaurant, so I had to add an option for that here.

MAKES ABOUT 22 FALAFELS TO SERVE 6 TO 7

- 2 green onions, roughly chopped
- ½ cup cilantro leaves and tender stems
- ½ cup parsley leaves and tender stems
- 3 (or 4, if you're a garlic lover!) garlic cloves, left whole
- 1½ cups dried split fava beans, soaked overnight (see Tip)
- 1½ teaspoons salt
- 1½ teaspoons ground coriander
- 1 teaspoon ground cumin
- ½ teaspoon freshly ground black pepper
- ¼ teaspoon cayenne pepper
- Vegetable oil, for deep-frying
- ¾ teaspoon baking soda
- 4 ounces mozzarella cheese (optional, for stuffing), cut into ½-inch cubes
- ¼ cup untoasted sesame seeds

In a food processor, combine the green onions, cilantro, parsley, and garlic. Blend until finely chopped. Add the drained fava beans and blend until the mixture is coarse but holds together when pressed. Do not overblend or it will become dense.

Transfer the mixture to a large bowl. Mix in the salt, coriander, cumin, black pepper, and cayenne. Cover and refrigerate for 30 minutes to 1 hour.

Line a plate with paper towels and have near the stove. Pour 2 to 3 inches of vegetable oil into a deep heavy-bottomed pot and heat to 350°F.

While the oil heats, line a baking sheet with parchment paper. Stir the baking soda into the falafel mixture. Using your hands or a large cookie scoop, scoop out about ¼-cup portions and shape into small balls or patties, 1½ to 2 inches wide, and place on the lined baking sheet.

Optional: If you want to stuff your falafel, flatten each slightly, place a cheese cube in the center, then seal the mixture around the cheese.

Lightly sprinkle the sesame seeds around the falafel. If you want them completely coated, then gently roll each piece in the seeds instead.

Working in batches to avoid overcrowding, fry the falafel, turning occasionally, until deep golden brown and crispy, 4 to 5 minutes. Use a spider or slotted spoon to transfer to paper towels to drain. Serve hot.

MORIBYAN'S TIP

To prepare the fava beans, rinse and dry them under cold water two times. Place them in a large bowl and add water to cover by at least 3 inches. Soak for at least 10 hours or overnight. Drain and rinse well before using.

THE CRISPIEST TRUFFLE PARMESAN ROAST POTATOES

When I visited the United Kingdom, I tried my first "Sunday roast," and what really blew me away were the potatoes. Usually I'm not into oven-baked potatoes. They're never crispy enough, and I always wish they were fries instead. But these were fluffy inside, perfectly crisp on the outside, and absolutely addictive. The trick is simple: Parboil the potatoes with a little baking soda, then shake them to rough up the edges. This creates a fluffy texture on the outside, almost like a thin coating of mashed potatoes. Then roast them in sizzling fat so the coating fries into a golden, crunchy crust. Duck fat is the most traditional and flavorful, but you can swap in ghee or a neutral oil if you prefer. These potatoes changed my life, and they'll change yours, too!

SERVES 4 TO 6

- Salt
- ½ teaspoon baking soda
- 2½ pounds russet or Yukon Gold potatoes, peeled and cut into 2- to 3-inch chunks
- ⅓ cup duck fat
- 6 garlic cloves
- 1 teaspoon truffle oil
- ¼ cup freshly grated Parmesan cheese

Bring a large pot of water to a boil. Add 1 tablespoon salt, the baking soda, and potato chunks. Parboil until the edges are just starting to soften but the centers are still firm, 8 to 10 minutes.

Drain thoroughly in a colander and let them steam-dry for a couple of minutes. Then shake the potatoes gently in the colander or pot to create rough, textured edges. These rough bits will crisp up beautifully in the oven.

Preheat the oven to 425°F. Place the duck fat and garlic cloves in a 9 × 13-inch roasting pan and heat in the oven until the fat is sizzling hot, 5 to 7 minutes.

Remove the pan from the oven and carefully add the potatoes to the hot duck fat, ensuring they sizzle on contact. Season lightly with salt and use a spoon or silicone spatula to toss them around and coat evenly.

Roast for 45 to 55 minutes, flipping the potatoes every 15 to 20 minutes to ensure even crisping on all sides. They should be golden brown and irresistibly crunchy on the outside, with a fluffy interior.

Remove the pan from the oven, discard the garlic, and toss the potatoes with the truffle oil, Parmesan, and salt to taste. Serve immediately and watch them disappear!

MORIBYAN'S TIP

If you're cutting your potatoes more than 30 minutes in advance of boiling, place them in a bowl of cold water so they don't oxidize.

LIBYAN EMBATTAN
(Fried Potatoes Stuffed with Beef)

Let me introduce you to everyone's favorite Libyan dish, embattan, also called batata embatna. It's a crispy potato pocket stuffed with spiced ground beef and fried to golden perfection. There are many different ways to make it: Some cook the beef first, some bread only the exposed part, some fry right after dipping in flour like I do, while my mother-in-law fries after dipping in egg. Others bake the potatoes in tomato sauce after frying. However you do it, it's all equally delicious and satisfying. If this recipe is the first thing you try from Libyan cuisine, get ready because it won't be the last.

MAKES ABOUT 16 TO SERVE 8

MEAT FILLING

- 2 tablespoons olive oil
- ½ small yellow onion, finely diced
- 1½ teaspoons finely minced garlic
- ½ pound ground beef (80/20)
- 1 tablespoon tomato paste
- 1 teaspoon paprika
- ½ teaspoon ground coriander
- ½ teaspoon ground ginger
- ¼ teaspoon ground turmeric
- ⅛ teaspoon cayenne pepper, or to taste
- ½ teaspoon salt
- ¼ teaspoon freshly ground black pepper
- 2 tablespoons finely chopped fresh cilantro
- 2 tablespoons finely chopped fresh parsley

STUFFED POTATOES

- 3 medium russet potatoes (1½ to 2 pounds)
- ½ cup all-purpose flour
- ½ cup fine dried bread crumbs
- 2 tablespoons cornstarch
- 1 teaspoon salt
- ½ teaspoon freshly ground black pepper
- 4 large eggs
- Vegetable oil, for deep-frying

Make the meat filling: In a skillet, heat the olive oil over medium heat. Add the onion and cook until softened, 3 to 4 minutes. Stir in the garlic and cook for 1 minute more. Add the ground beef, tomato paste, all the spices, and the salt and pepper and cook until the meat is browned and fully cooked through, 7 to 8 minutes.

Stir in the cilantro and parsley. Transfer the mixture to a bowl, cover, and refrigerate for at least 1 hour, or until chilled and firm enough to hold together when stuffed into the potatoes.

Stuff and fry the potatoes: Peel each potato and arrange it horizontally on a cutting board. Now, you are going to cut the potato crosswise into discs with a pocket in the middle like a clamshell. To do this, make your first cut about ½ centimeter from the edge of the potato, but don't slice all the way through the potato—just about three-quarters of the way down (this will be your pocket). Now, ½ centimeter away from that first cut, slice all the way through the potato. You should have a clamshell-like disc that is 1 centimeter (a scant ½ inch) thick. Continue this process until all potatoes are sliced into clamshells.

Set up a dredging station in two large bowls: In one bowl, combine the flour, bread crumbs, cornstarch, ½ teaspoon of the salt, and ¼ teaspoon of the black pepper. Mix well. In a second bowl, whisk together the eggs, remaining ½ teaspoon salt, and remaining ¼ teaspoon black pepper.

RECIPE & INGREDIENTS CONTINUE

Carefully open each potato slice and stuff it with 1 to 2 tablespoons of the prepared meat filling, making sure to fill the pocket without overstuffing. Repeat this for all the potato slices.

Dredge each stuffed potato slice in the flour/bread crumb mixture, ensuring it is well coated on all sides. Then, dip it into the egg mixture. At this point, you can fry them straight from the egg wash (the way my mother-in-law makes them), or for extra crunch, coat once again in the flour/bread crumb mixture before frying. Repeat with all the stuffed potato slices.

Set a wire rack in a sheet pan and have near the stove. Pour 2 inches of vegetable oil into a deep heavy-bottomed pot or Dutch oven and heat over medium heat to 325°F.

Working in batches to avoid overcrowding, fry the embattan until golden brown and crispy on all sides, turning occasionally. Fry for about 10 minutes if you plan to finish baking them in tomato sauce, or 15 to 18 minutes if you are serving them straight from the fryer. Once fried, remove the embattan and place them on the wire rack to drain the excess oil.

Optional, bake in tomato sauce: Preheat the oven to 375°F.

Arrange the fried embattan in a single layer in a large baking dish. In a bowl, whisk together the tomato paste, ½ cup water, salt, pepper, and garlic powder. Pour evenly over the potatoes. Bake uncovered for 20 to 25 minutes, until bubbling and the flavors have melded.

Allow to cool for a few minutes before enjoying warm!

TOMATO SAUCE (OPTIONAL)

2 tablespoons tomato paste
¼ teaspoon salt
¼ teaspoon freshly ground black pepper
¼ teaspoon garlic powder

CRISPIEST FRIED CALAMARI

I've never been a big seafood person, but crispy fried calamari is the one thing I'll always make an exception for. My dad would order it every single time we went out to eat, and eventually I gave in and tried it. One bite turned into five, and the rest was history. Now if you leave me alone with a plate, I might just clear it on my own. It's so addictive and honestly not that fishy. Just add a squeeze of lemon and your favorite dipping sauce, and you've got the perfect appetizer.

SERVES 4

1 pound fresh calamari, cleaned, with tubes sliced into rings
¼ cup fresh lemon juice
1 tablespoon olive oil
Salt
1 cup all-purpose flour
½ cup cornstarch
1 teaspoon baking powder
½ teaspoon freshly ground black pepper
½ teaspoon paprika
½ teaspoon garlic powder
½ teaspoon onion powder
½ teaspoon mustard powder
¾ cup buttermilk
1 large egg
Neutral oil, for deep-frying
Lemon wedges, for serving
Tartar sauce or your favorite dipping sauce, for serving

In a bowl or ziplock bag, combine the calamari, lemon juice, olive oil, and a pinch of salt. Cover and let it sit for 1 hour in the refrigerator to tenderize.

Drain the calamari and pat dry with a paper towel.

In a large bowl, whisk together the flour, cornstarch, baking powder, 1 teaspoon salt, the black pepper, paprika, garlic powder, onion powder, and mustard powder.

In a medium bowl or another ziplock bag, whisk together the buttermilk with the egg. Add 3 to 4 tablespoons of the buttermilk mixture to the flour mixture and massage in with your hands to create a flaky texture.

Submerge all the calamari in the buttermilk mixture. Use your hands or tongs to pull out the calamari from the wet batter, piece by piece, letting the buttermilk drip off. Toss the rings in the flour mixture until very well coated (inside the ring, too!), shaking off any excess flour.

Set a wire rack in a sheet pan and have near the stove. Pour 2 to 3 inches neutral oil into a deep-fryer or heavy-bottomed pot and heat over medium heat until it reaches 350°F.

Working in batches to avoid overcrowding, fry the calamari until golden brown and crispy, 2 to 3 minutes per batch. Remove with a slotted spoon and drain on the wire rack.

Sprinkle with additional salt if desired and squeeze lemon juice on top. Serve with additional lemon wedges on the side, plus tartar sauce or your favorite dipping sauce.

DYNAMITE SHRIMP BAO BUNS

This recipe is inspired by one of my favorite restaurants in Philadelphia called Buddakan. The crispy, sweet, and spicy shrimp paired with soft, pillowy bao completely blew my mind! I knew I had to re-create it at home. This version is a little different from the volcano shrimp you might've seen on my blog because it swaps out the panko coating for a light, airy tempura batter. When done right, tempura is a game changer: It puffs up, crisps perfectly, and practically shatters in your mouth. The key? Getting that oil temperature just right. If you're not careful and the oil dips too low, you'll end up with soggy, greasy shrimp. So, be patient and give the oil time to come back to temp between batches. Trust me, it's worth the wait!

MAKES 14 TO 16 BAO TO SERVE 6

DYNAMITE SAUCE

- ½ cup mayonnaise
- ½ cup Thai sweet chili sauce
- 2 teaspoons rice vinegar
- 1 teaspoon sriracha
- 1 teaspoon minced garlic
- ¼ teaspoon freshly ground black pepper

TEMPURA SHRIMP

- ⅔ cup all-purpose flour
- ⅓ cup cornstarch
- 1½ teaspoons salt
- 1 teaspoon baking powder
- 1 teaspoon paprika
- 1 teaspoon chili powder
- ½ teaspoon freshly ground black pepper
- ½ teaspoon garlic powder
- 1 pound medium shrimp, peeled and deveined
- ⅔ cup cold club soda
- 1 large egg
- Vegetable oil, for deep-frying

ASSEMBLY

- Pillowy Bao Buns, warmed (page 221)
- Thinly sliced cucumber
- Chopped green onions or sesame seeds (optional), for garnish
- Sriracha (optional)

Make the dynamite sauce: In a small bowl, mix together the mayonnaise, sweet chili sauce, rice vinegar, sriracha, garlic, and black pepper. Set aside.

Make the tempura shrimp: In a bowl, whisk together the flour, cornstarch, salt, baking powder, paprika, chili powder, black pepper, and garlic powder.

Coat the shrimp in the dry mixture, then transfer to a plate.

Add the club soda and egg to the remaining dry mixture, whisking until just combined. Avoid overmixing.

Line a baking sheet with a wire rack or paper towels and have near the stove. Pour 2 inches of vegetable oil into a deep heavy-bottomed pan and heat to 350°F.

Working in batches to avoid overcrowding, dip each shrimp into the tempura batter, letting any excess drip off. Carefully place the shrimp into the hot oil and fry until golden and crispy, 4 to 6 minutes. Transfer to the wire rack or paper towels to drain.

Once all the shrimp are fried and drained, transfer to a bowl and toss them in the prepared dynamite sauce until well coated.

Assemble: Gently open the warm bao buns. Add a few slices of fresh cucumber to each. Place 2 to 3 tempura shrimp inside each bun. If desired, garnish with chopped green onions or sesame seeds and add more sriracha.

SOUPS & STEWS

MAMA NEZHA'S LENTIL SOUP

When it's time to break our fasts during the month of Ramadan, soup is always the first thing on the table before the main meal. My mom has a few recipes she rotates, but this lentil soup—*sharbat addis* in Arabic—has always been one of my favorites. I learned how to make it in my first Ramadan after getting married, when I was away from home and longing for the traditions I grew up with. Some people add vegetables like zucchini or potato to make it heartier, but I prefer it the way my mom makes it, with just a few ingredients and a clean, comforting flavor. It can also easily be made vegetarian by swapping in vegetable broth.

SERVES 6 TO 8

- 3 tablespoons extra-virgin olive oil
- ½ yellow onion, finely diced
- 2 teaspoons minced garlic
- ⅔ cup shredded or grated carrots
- 1½ cups red lentils, rinsed and drained
- 1¼ teaspoons freshly ground black pepper
- 1 teaspoon ground turmeric
- 1 teaspoon ground cumin, or more to taste
- ¾ to 1 teaspoon salt, to taste
- 4 cups chicken broth
- ½ teaspoon red pepper flakes, plus more for garnish
- Lemon wedges, for serving
- Crispy bread or pita chips, for serving

In a large pot or Dutch oven, warm the olive oil over medium heat. Once hot, add the diced onion, garlic, and carrots and cook, stirring occasionally, until the onions are soft and lightly golden and the carrots have begun to soften, 6 to 7 minutes.

Add the lentils and stir for 2 to 3 minutes, letting them toast slightly and absorb the flavor of the aromatics.

Sprinkle in the black pepper, turmeric, cumin, and salt. Stir well to coat everything evenly in the spices and let cook for another minute to let the flavors bloom.

Pour in the chicken broth and 2 cups water and bring to a boil. Reduce the heat to low, cover, and let the soup simmer until the lentils are completely softened and the soup is thickened, 45 to 50 minutes.

Once everything is tender, remove the pot from the heat. Use an immersion blender to blend the soup directly in the pot until smooth and creamy. (Alternatively, to use a regular blender, allow the soup to cool slightly for 10 to 15 minutes. Carefully transfer it in batches to a blender, filling it only halfway each time to prevent overflow. Remove the center cap of the lid to let steam escape, cover with a clean kitchen towel, and blend until smooth.)

Add pepper flakes to round out the flavor and taste the soup and adjust any other seasoning as needed—add more cumin if you'd like a deeper flavor. The consistency should also be perfect but if it happens to be too thick, add a splash of water to thin it out.

Serve hot with a generous squeeze of lemon and a sprinkle of red pepper flakes. Pair with crispy bread or pita chips for dipping.

CREAMY ROASTED RED PEPPER & TOMATO SOUP

This soup was my go-to comfort meal in college, except back then I'd grab a carton from the grocery store and zhuzh it up with some freshly grated Parmesan and olive oil. It always hit the spot! But once I had a proper kitchen of my own, I realized how easy it is to make a way better version from scratch. Roasting the tomatoes and peppers before blending them deepens their flavor and adds a subtle char that is so simple but so much better than anything in a carton or can. Pair it with your favorite grilled cheese, or just top with Parm, a drizzle of cream, and some crusty bread for the perfect meal.

SERVES 6

- 2 red bell peppers, halved and seeded
- 9 medium tomatoes (about 2½ pounds total), cut into quarters
- ½ large yellow onion, roughly chopped
- 3 tablespoons olive oil, plus more for drizzling
- Salt and freshly ground black pepper
- 1 tablespoon unsalted butter
- 3 tablespoons tomato paste
- 1 tablespoon minced garlic
- 1 cup vegetable or chicken broth
- ½ cup whole milk
- ¼ cup heavy cream, plus more for garnish
- 6 fresh basil leaves, plus more for garnish
- 1 teaspoon dried thyme
- ½ cup freshly grated Parmesan cheese, plus more for serving
- 2 teaspoons sugar (optional, to balance acidity)
- Dash of cayenne pepper or red pepper flakes, or to taste
- 1 teaspoon Worcestershire sauce

Preheat the oven to 425°F.

Place the bell peppers cut-side down, the tomatoes cut-side up, and the onion on a large sheet pan. Drizzle with olive oil and season with a pinch of salt and pepper. Roast until the bell pepper skins are charred and the vegetables are tender, 35 to 40 minutes.

In a large pot, heat the 3 tablespoons olive oil and butter over medium heat. Once the oil is hot, add the tomato paste and garlic and sauté until deeper in color and fragrant, 2 to 3 minutes.

Add the roasted vegetables to the pot along with the broth, milk, heavy cream, basil leaves, and thyme. Use an immersion blender to puree until smooth. (Alternatively, transfer in batches to a high-powered blender and puree until smooth and return to the pot.) If you'd like, you can run the soup through a fine-mesh sieve for an even smoother texture, but this is totally optional.

Stir in the grated Parmesan cheese, sugar (if using), 1 teaspoon salt, ½ teaspoon black pepper, cayenne, and Worcestershire sauce. Let the soup simmer for 10 to 15 minutes more, to allow the flavors to meld. Taste and adjust the seasoning with additional salt, black pepper, or cayenne if needed.

Ladle the soup into bowls and garnish with additional Parmesan cheese, fresh basil leaves, or a drizzle of cream or olive oil. Serve warm.

MORIBYAN'S TIP

If tomatoes are not in season, the tomatoes you find in stores might have a more muted flavor. In this case, add more tomato paste, or use a blend of cherry and Roma tomatoes.

CHICKEN NOODLE SOUP
with Homemade Noodles

There's nothing better than when you're feeling sick and someone brings you a warm bowl of soup. It's even better when it's made from scratch; it's like an "I love you" in a bowl. This soup is thick and creamy, not just a thin broth with noodles and veggies. I season it with red pepper flakes to add depth, plus a touch of nutmeg and lemon juice for brightness. The real stars are the homemade egg noodles. Making noodles from scratch might sound like a lot of work but they come together easily with just a rolling pin and some elbow grease. At the end of the day the most important ingredient in this soup is love. It's what turns a simple meal into something truly comforting and special.

SERVES 6 TO 8

HOMEMADE EGG NOODLES

1¾ cups all-purpose flour, plus more for dusting
1 teaspoon salt
2 large eggs, beaten
3 tablespoons milk

SOUP

2 tablespoons unsalted butter
1 tablespoon olive oil
3 large carrots, diced
½ yellow onion, diced
3 celery stalks, diced
1 tablespoon minced garlic
5 cups low-sodium chicken broth
2 cups half-and-half
¼ cup all-purpose flour
12 ounces shredded rotisserie chicken
½ teaspoon freshly ground black pepper
1 teaspoon lemon pepper
1 teaspoon dried thyme
1 teaspoon dried oregano
1 teaspoon paprika
½ to 1 teaspoon red pepper flakes, to taste
½ teaspoon salt, or to taste
2 chicken bouillon cubes
Dash of ground nutmeg
½ cup grated Parmesan cheese, plus more to taste
Squeeze of fresh lemon juice, for finishing
2 tablespoons chopped fresh parsley

Make the egg noodles: In a large bowl, whisk together the flour and salt.

In a separate bowl, whisk the eggs and milk together until smooth. Gradually pour the egg and milk mixture into the flour mixture, stirring to form a rough dough.

Turn the dough out onto a floured surface and knead until smooth and elastic, 5 to 7 minutes. Wrap the dough in plastic and let it rest at room temperature for at least 30 minutes and up to 3 days.

Dust your surface with flour again. Roll the dough out very thin (about ⅛ inch thick). Cut into thin strips (no more than ¼ inch wide) to form noodles. Lightly dust the noodles with flour to prevent sticking. Cover and set aside.

Make the soup: In a large pot or Dutch oven, melt the butter with the olive oil over medium heat. Add the carrots, onion, and celery and sauté until the vegetables are softened and lightly golden, 5 to 7 minutes. Stir in the garlic and cook for 30 seconds, just until fragrant. Pour in the chicken broth, stirring to combine with the vegetables.

In a small bowl or cup, whisk the half-and-half with the flour until completely smooth. Pour the mixture into the pot, stirring constantly to create a creamy base.

Stir in the shredded chicken, black pepper, lemon pepper, thyme, oregano, paprika, pepper flakes, salt, bouillon cubes, nutmeg, and Parmesan.

Bring the soup to a gentle simmer and cook for 10 minutes to allow the flavors to meld. Drop in the homemade egg noodles and simmer until the noodles are tender, 2 to 3 minutes.

Finish the soup with a squeeze of fresh lemon juice and stir in the chopped parsley. Taste and adjust seasoning as needed. Serve hot.

LIBYAN FASOLIA

(White Bean & Tomato Stew with Lamb)

In Libya, where my dad is from, this is called fasolia; in Morocco, my mom's home country, it is called loubia. Either way, it's a simple one-pot stew of beans, tender lamb, and a North African blend of warming spices like ginger and cumin. Different regions and families have different ways of making it; my mom's stew was always on the thicker side, which is how I like it, and my father likes it on the spicier side. When I asked her how she made it, her "measurements" were: Add water until it looks right, one big spoon of this, one small spoon of that. After lots of trial and error, I finally landed on a version that got her stamp of approval. I hope you love it as much as I do.

SERVES 4 TO 6

3 tablespoons olive oil
½ yellow onion, finely chopped
¼ cup tomato paste
2 teaspoons minced garlic
1½ pounds lamb stew meat, cut into bite-size pieces
2 teaspoons paprika
1½ teaspoons salt, or more to taste
1 teaspoon ground ginger
1 teaspoon ground cumin
1 teaspoon ground turmeric
½ teaspoon freshly ground black pepper
¼ teaspoon cayenne pepper, or more to taste
2 tomatoes, grated on the large holes of a box grater
2 (15-ounce) cans white beans, drained and rinsed
1 tablespoon all-purpose flour
1 tablespoon chopped fresh parsley
1 tablespoon chopped fresh cilantro
Lemon wedges, for serving
Bread, for serving

In a large soup pot or Dutch oven, heat the oil over medium heat. Add the onion and cook, stirring occasionally, until soft and translucent, 6 to 8 minutes.

Add the tomato paste and garlic and cook for 2 to 3 minutes, stirring constantly. This helps deepen the flavor and remove the raw, acidic taste. The color should darken slightly and the paste will start to caramelize.

Add the lamb and season with the paprika, salt, ginger, cumin, turmeric, black pepper, and cayenne. Toss to coat in the tomato paste and spices, then cook until the meat is browned on all sides, 6 to 8 minutes.

Stir in the grated tomatoes and cook until the mixture thickens slightly and the tomatoes break down, 3 to 4 more minutes.

Pour in 3 cups water and bring to a boil. Reduce the heat to low, cover, and simmer, stirring occasionally, until the lamb is tender, 1½ to 2 hours.

Add the white beans and cook uncovered for 20 minutes.

Scoop ¼ cup of the broth from the pot into a small bowl. Add the flour and mix until smooth, then stir the mixture back into the pot. Simmer until the sauce has thickened, 4 to 5 more minutes.

Turn off the heat and stir in the parsley and cilantro. Serve with lemons for squeezing and bread to dip and scoop!

LASAGNA SOUP

What's better than soup? Soup that's actually pasta in disguise! This concept went viral a while ago, and once I realized I could enjoy all the comforting flavors of lasagna without the hassle of layering noodles or waiting forever for it to bake, I was hooked. This version tastes just like the classic lasagna, though I might even prefer it to the baked version. While some lasagna soups can be too thin, this one is rich, thick, and hearty—more like a stew. Turns out, lasagna is even better when you can dive into it with a spoon!

SERVES 6

RICOTTA TOPPING

- 1½ cups whole-milk ricotta cheese
- ⅓ cup grated Parmesan cheese
- Pinch of nutmeg
- Salt and freshly ground black pepper

SOUP

- 1 tablespoon olive oil
- 1 tablespoon unsalted butter
- 1 tablespoon minced garlic
- 1 pound ground beef (90/10)
- 1½ teaspoons Italian seasoning
- 1½ teaspoons paprika
- 1 teaspoon red pepper flakes, or to taste
- ½ teaspoon onion powder
- ½ teaspoon garlic powder
- ½ teaspoon dried oregano
- ½ teaspoon freshly ground black pepper
- ½ teaspoon salt, or to taste
- 1 (24-ounce) jar marinara sauce
- 4 cups beef broth
- ½ cup heavy cream
- 12 ounces lasagna sheets, broken into 1- to 2-inch pieces
- ⅓ cup shredded mozzarella cheese, or to taste
- 2 tablespoons chopped fresh basil
- 2 tablespoons finely chopped fresh parsley
- ¼ to ⅓ cup freshly grated Parmesan cheese, to taste

Make the ricotta topping: In a small bowl, mix together the ricotta, Parmesan, nutmeg, and salt and pepper to taste until smooth. Set aside.

Make the soup: In a large pot, heat the olive oil, butter, and garlic over medium-high heat. Sauté until the garlic is fragrant, 1 to 2 minutes. Add the ground beef and season with the Italian seasoning, paprika, pepper flakes, onion powder, garlic powder, oregano, black pepper, and salt. Using a wooden spoon to break up the meat into small pieces, mix and cook until the meat is browned and broken up completely, 8 to 9 minutes.

Add the marinara sauce, beef broth, and heavy cream. Mix well and bring to a slow boil.

Add the broken lasagna sheets and cook until the pasta is fully cooked and softened, 15 to 16 minutes.

Finally, mix the mozzarella, basil, parsley, and Parmesan into the soup. Serve warm in a bowl with dollops of the seasoned ricotta on top to enjoy!

JAPANESE-STYLE BEEF CURRY STEW

This dish is the definition of comfort food. Whenever I'm feeling sick or it's a cold, rainy day, this is exactly what I crave. When my sisters and I visited Japan, we wasted no time. We arrived late, went straight from the airport to the hotel to drop off our bags, then immediately set out to find a curry restaurant that was still open. If you've never had Japanese curry before, it's thicker than an Indian or Thai curry, with a sweeter flavor and a more gentle heat. The S&B brand Japanese curry powder and roux I call for here are widely available in most grocery stores.

SERVES 6 TO 8

1½ pounds chuck roast, cut into bite-size pieces
2 teaspoons Japanese curry powder
1½ tablespoons cornstarch
¾ teaspoon salt
½ teaspoon freshly ground black pepper
1 tablespoon unsalted butter
3 tablespoons neutral oil
1 large yellow onion, thinly sliced
2 tablespoons ketchup
1 tablespoon minced garlic
2 teaspoons ginger paste
4 cups low-sodium beef broth
1 tablespoon Worcestershire sauce
1 tablespoon reduced-sodium soy sauce
3 carrots, cut into chunks
2 small potatoes (or 1 large), peeled and cut into chunks
2 tablespoons heavy cream
1½ tablespoons honey
1 (3.2-ounce) package mild Japanese curry roux
¼ to ½ teaspoon cayenne powder, to taste
Steamed white rice, for serving
Fukujinzuke (Japanese pickled veggies), for serving

In a medium bowl, toss the beef with the curry powder, cornstarch, salt, and pepper until evenly coated.

In a large pot or Dutch oven, melt the butter over medium-high heat. Add 1 tablespoon of the neutral oil. Working in batches, sear the beef until deeply browned all over, 3 to 4 minutes per side. Remove from the pot and set aside.

In the same pot (no need to clean it), heat the remaining 2 tablespoons neutral oil over medium heat. Add the onion and cook, stirring occasionally, until caramelized and deep golden brown, 15 to 20 minutes.

Stir in the ketchup, garlic, and ginger paste, cooking for another minute until fragrant.

Pour in the beef broth, Worcestershire sauce, and soy sauce, scraping the bottom of the pot to deglaze. Return the seared beef to the pot. Cover and let it simmer for 50 minutes.

Uncover the pot and add the carrots. Stir well and continue cooking, covered, for 15 more minutes.

Add the potatoes, cover again, and cook until both the potatoes and carrots are tender, about 30 minutes.

Uncover and stir in the heavy cream, honey, and curry roux until fully dissolved. Add the cayenne for a touch of heat. Let the curry simmer for a few more minutes until thickened and rich.

Enjoy warm with steamed rice and fukujinzuke.

SHEET PAN, ONE-POT & 30-MINUTE MEALS

PAD KEE MAO
(Drunken Noodles with Chicken)

Thai food is easily my favorite cuisine, and while we all know and love pad Thai and pad see ew, pad kee mao deserves way more attention than it gets. This dish hits the perfect sweet and spicy notes with a great crunch from bell peppers and Chinese broccoli. I usually make it with chicken, but tofu, shrimp, or beef all work great. Also, did I mention it comes together in under thirty minutes?

SERVES 4

- 1 pound fresh wide rice noodle sheets (see Tip)
- 2 tablespoons oyster sauce
- 2 tablespoons dark soy sauce
- 1 tablespoon soy sauce
- 2 teaspoons fish sauce
- 2 tablespoons brown or palm sugar
- 1 tablespoon rice vinegar
- ¼ teaspoon ground white pepper, plus more to taste
- 2 tablespoons neutral oil
- 12 ounces boneless, skinless chicken thighs, thinly sliced
- Salt
- 1 tablespoon minced garlic
- 3 to 4 Thai chiles, seeded and finely chopped
- ½ red bell pepper, thinly sliced
- 5 ounces Chinese broccoli, chopped into bite-size pieces (1½ cups), leaves and stem pieces kept separate
- 2 handfuls Thai basil (about 1 cup), larger leaves torn

Cut the rice noodle sheets into 1-inch-wide strips. Gently separate the strips—they can stick together, especially if cold. To help them loosen up, warm them in the microwave in 1-minute intervals, for 2 to 3 minutes total, until softened. (Alternatively, you can soak them in hot water for 3 to 4 minutes until soft and pliable.)

In a small bowl, whisk together the oyster sauce, dark soy sauce, regular soy sauce, fish sauce, brown sugar, vinegar, 1 tablespoon water, and the white pepper. Set aside.

Heat a wok or large skillet over medium-high heat. Add 1 tablespoon of the oil and the sliced chicken. Season lightly with salt and white pepper. Stir-fry until fully cooked and golden on the edges, 4 to 5 minutes. Remove the chicken from the pan and set aside.

Add the remaining 1 tablespoon oil to the pan. Add the garlic and Thai chiles and stir-fry for 30 seconds until fragrant. Add the bell pepper and Chinese broccoli stems. Cook until the stems begin to soften, for 2 minutes. Add the Chinese broccoli leaves and cook until wilted and vibrant green, 1 to 2 more minutes.

Add the softened noodles to the pan, followed by the cooked chicken and sauce. Toss everything gently for 2 to 3 minutes until the noodles are evenly coated, glossy, and the sauce slightly thickens.

Add the Thai basil and toss until wilted and fragrant, 30 seconds to 1 minute. Enjoy immediately while everything is still warm!

MORIBYAN'S TIP

Fresh wide rice noodle sheets typically come shrink-wrapped or in sealed plastic bags, with thick, pliable sheets stacked on top of each other and stored in liquid. Look for them at most Asian markets, especially those specializing in Southeast Asian cuisine. After you microwave or soak them, they don't need to be cooked further; the noodles will finish in the wok and soak up the sauce beautifully.

EASIEST UDON STIR-FRY
with Steak

My sisters and I always loved cooking Asian-inspired food at home, and one of the first dishes I learned from them was a noodle stir-fry. This meal comes together quickly in one pan. In this recipe, the veggies and steak get stir-fried and kissed with that delicious wok hei flavor, a.k.a. the smoky, caramelized notes that come from high-heat wok cooking. I use thick and chewy udon noodles, but you can easily swap in any noodles you like, such as lo mein. You can also customize the vegetables with what you have on hand and add any protein you like, such as shrimp, chicken, or even tofu.

SERVES 2 TO 4

SAUCE

- 2 tablespoons dark soy sauce
- 2 tablespoons oyster sauce
- 1½ tablespoons brown sugar
- 1 tablespoon rice vinegar
- 1 teaspoon toasted sesame oil
- 1 teaspoon red pepper flakes
- ½ teaspoon freshly ground black pepper

STEAK AND UDON

- 1 pound rib-eye steak, thinly sliced against the grain
- 2 tablespoons cornstarch
- 1 tablespoon dark soy sauce
- ½ teaspoon baking soda
- ½ teaspoon freshly ground black pepper
- ¼ teaspoon salt
- 17.6 ounces (500g) fresh, frozen, or cooked dried udon noodles (see Tip)

STIR-FRY

- 3 tablespoons neutral oil, plus more if needed
- ½ yellow onion, chopped
- 2 cups thinly sliced cabbage
- 1 cup matchstick carrots
- 1 tablespoon minced garlic
- 4 green onions, green parts only, chopped into chunks

Make the sauce: In a small bowl, whisk together the dark soy sauce, oyster sauce, brown sugar, rice vinegar, sesame oil, pepper flakes, black pepper, and 2 tablespoons water. Set the sauce aside.

Prepare the steak and udon: In a bowl, toss the sliced rib eye with the cornstarch, dark soy sauce, baking soda, black pepper, and salt. Let it marinate briefly while prepping the rest.

Cook the udon noodles according to package instructions (usually boiling for about 1 minute). Drain and set aside.

Prepare the stir-fry: Heat a wok or large sauté pan over medium-high heat for a few minutes until hot. Add the neutral oil and, once hot, add the beef and sear until browned and just cooked through, 3 to 4 minutes. Remove and set aside on a plate.

Do not clean the wok or pan, but if it looks dry, add up to 1 tablespoon of oil to it. Add the onion, cabbage, and carrots all together. Stir-fry until the vegetables are tender-crisp and caramelized a bit, 5 to 6 minutes. Stir in the garlic and cook until fragrant, about 30 seconds.

Return the cooked beef to the pan along with the green onions and cooked udon noodles. Pour the sauce over everything and toss well to coat. Cook until heated through, 2 to 3 minutes. Serve warm to enjoy!

MORIBYAN'S TIP

At many grocery stores, you can find fresh or frozen udon (in the refrigerated section near the tofu or in the freezer aisle, respectively). This is what I love to use for this dish. However, if all you can find is dried udon, cook it according to the package instructions and proceed with the recipe.

ONE-PAN ALFREDO ORZO

with Chicken & Spinach

For the longest time, I honestly thought orzo was just a thicker, chewier version of rice. But fun fact, it's actually pasta! Once I realized that, everything clicked. I always tossed it into rice dishes, but this time I wanted to try something different. So, I decided to fuse it with a classic pasta dish, fettuccine Alfredo, because at the end of the day, orzo is pasta, whether it looks like it or not. The creamy, garlicky, cheesy sauce clings to each piece in the best way, giving you all the cozy comfort of the original dish, just in a lighter, silkier form.

SERVES 4

CHICKEN

- 2 tablespoons olive oil
- 2 teaspoons Italian seasoning
- 1 teaspoon smoked paprika
- ¾ teaspoon salt
- ½ teaspoon garlic powder
- ½ teaspoon dried oregano
- ½ teaspoon freshly ground black pepper
- 1 pound boneless, skinless chicken breasts (2 to 3 pieces)

ALFREDO ORZO

- 1 tablespoon unsalted butter
- 1 tablespoon olive oil
- 1 tablespoon minced garlic
- 1⅓ cups orzo
- 2¼ cups chicken broth
- ½ teaspoon salt
- ¼ teaspoon freshly ground black pepper
- ½ cup heavy cream
- ½ cup grated Parmesan cheese, plus more for serving
- Pinch of nutmeg
- 1½ cups fresh baby spinach
- 1½ teaspoons chopped fresh parsley
- Grated zest of 1 lemon

Cook the chicken: In a medium bowl, stir together 1 tablespoon of the olive oil, the Italian seasoning, smoked paprika, salt, garlic powder, oregano, and black pepper. Add the chicken and turn to coat evenly.

In a skillet, heat the remaining 1 tablespoon olive oil over medium heat. Add the chicken and cook until golden brown and fully cooked, 4 to 5 minutes per side depending on the thickness of the breast. Remove and set aside.

Make the Alfredo orzo: In the same pan, add the olive oil and melt the butter over medium heat. Add the garlic and cook until fragrant, 1 to 2 minutes. Stir in the orzo and toast until lightly golden, 1 to 2 minutes.

Pour in the chicken broth, season with the salt and black pepper, and bring to a boil. Turn the heat to low, cover, and cook until the orzo is tender and most of the liquid is absorbed, 12 to 15 minutes.

Uncover and stir in the heavy cream, Parmesan, and nutmeg until smooth. Add the spinach, mix again, and let it wilt, 1 to 2 minutes.

Slice the cooked chicken and serve it over the creamy orzo. Finish with a sprinkle of Parmesan, parsley, and lemon zest for a bright, fresh touch.

FRENCH ONION PASTA

This one-pot pasta is French onion soup reinvented. After you brown the onions to perfection, you add everything from broth and spices to the pasta in the same pot, letting it soak up all those rich, caramelized flavors. And if you want to take it to the next level (trust me, you do), transfer everything to a broiler-proof dish, sprinkle with shredded Gruyère, and finish under the heat until golden and bubbling. It's the ultimate cozy, indulgent meal that combines everything you love about French onion soup with the comfort of pasta.

SERVES 4

- 1 tablespoon olive oil
- 2 tablespoons unsalted butter
- 2 yellow onions, thinly sliced
- 1 tablespoon distilled white vinegar
- 1 tablespoon minced garlic
- 4 cups beef broth
- 1 tablespoon Worcestershire sauce
- 1 teaspoon dried thyme
- ¾ teaspoon smoked paprika
- ¾ teaspoon red pepper flakes
- ½ to ¾ teaspoon salt, to taste
- ½ teaspoon freshly ground black pepper, or more to taste
- 12 ounces pasta (rigatoni or fusilli work great)
- ⅓ cup heavy cream
- ¾ cup freshly grated Parmesan cheese
- 1 tablespoon chopped parsley
- Shredded Gruyère cheese (optional), for topping
- Crusty bread (optional), for serving

In a large pot, heat the oil and butter over medium heat. Once the butter has melted, add the onions and let them cook low and slow until they get golden, jammy, and packed with flavor, about 30 minutes. Stir every few minutes to make sure they brown evenly. You may need to reduce the heat to medium-low if they're cooking too quickly.

Pour in the vinegar to deglaze the pan, scraping up all those flavorful bits stuck at the bottom. Add the garlic and sauté for just a minute until fragrant.

Pour in the beef broth, Worcestershire sauce, thyme, smoked paprika, pepper flakes, salt, and black pepper. Stir it all together and add the pasta straight into the pot. Bring everything to a simmer and cook, uncovered, until the pasta is tender and has soaked up all that brothy goodness, about 20 minutes. Stir occasionally so nothing sticks to the bottom.

Once the pasta is cooked through and the sauce has thickened, lower the heat and stir in the heavy cream, Parmesan, and parsley. Mix until it's silky, creamy, and everything is coated in that cheesy onion sauce.

Optional but HIGHLY recommended broil step: Transfer the pasta to a broiler-proof dish, top with shredded Gruyère, and broil until melted and bubbling—just like the cheesy top on a bowl of French onion soup.

If desired, serve warm with crusty bread on the side to soak up every last drop of that rich, savory sauce.

POPEYE'S PASTA

I know parents are always looking for ways to get their kids to eat more veggies. Well, I'm a fully grown adult, and I still struggle to get my greens in. Inspired by Popeye and his love for spinach, I created this pasta sauce with a mix of leafy greens, herbs, and veggies that are all green, of course—kale, peas, basil, and spinach. If you ate this blindfolded without seeing the color, you'd never guess there are four different greens hiding in there. The sauce comes together with a little butter and cream and is finished with a dollop of ricotta, which is optional but so worth it. It's creamy and indulgent but also secretly good for you.

SERVES 4

- Salt
- 1 cup roughly chopped kale leaves (tough stems and midribs removed)
- 1¾ cups tightly packed fresh baby spinach
- 1¾ cups green peas, fresh or thawed frozen
- 4 fresh basil leaves
- 12 ounces medium pasta shells (or any pasta shape you like)
- 1 tablespoon olive oil, plus more for drizzling
- 1 tablespoon unsalted butter
- ½ yellow onion, finely diced
- 1½ teaspoons minced garlic
- 1 cup heavy cream
- ¾ cup freshly grated Parmesan cheese
- ½ teaspoon salt, plus more to taste
- ½ teaspoon freshly ground black pepper
- Whole-milk ricotta cheese (optional), for topping

Bring a large pot of salted water to a boil. Add the chopped kale and blanch for 60 seconds to soften. Use a slotted spoon to transfer it directly to a blender or food processor.

In the same pot of boiling water, add the spinach and 1 cup of the peas. Blanch for 30 seconds, then transfer the spinach and the peas directly to the blender with the kale. Save the blanching water in the pot—you'll use it to cook the pasta.

Add the basil leaves to the blender and blend the greens mixture until smooth and vibrant. If it's not blending easily, you can add a small splash of water (about 1 tablespoon), but you likely won't need it. Set aside.

To the same pot with the blanching water, add more water as needed, bring it back to a boil, and cook the pasta according to package instructions. Before draining, reserve ½ cup of the cooking water.

While the pasta cooks, make the sauce. In a large skillet, heat the olive oil and butter over medium heat. Add the diced onion and sauté until soft and translucent, 2 to 3 minutes. Stir in the garlic and cook until fragrant, 30 seconds.

Pour in the pureed greens and stir to combine. Add the heavy cream and continue stirring until the sauce is smooth and warmed through.

Add the pasta water, Parmesan, salt, and black pepper to the sauce. Stir and let simmer for 2 to 3 minutes to slightly thicken. Taste and adjust with more salt if needed.

Add the cooked pasta shells to the skillet and toss until well coated. Fold in the reserved cooked peas and let everything simmer together for about 2 more minutes.

Plate and finish with a drizzle of olive oil. For extra creaminess, top with small dollops of fresh ricotta cheese, if desired.

BABA'S MBAKBAKA
(One-Pot Libyan Pasta)

Mbakbaka is one of the most iconic Libyan dishes, not just for its unique name but also for its flavor. It's a one-pot pasta cooked in a rich tomato broth with lamb and onions, and it's surprisingly easy to make. The hardest part is simply waiting for the lamb to get tender. And fun fact, the name comes from the sound it makes—*bak bak*—just like the broth bubbling and popping as the lamb and pasta cook.

My dad taught this recipe to my mom when they first got married, and later he passed it down to me. On camping trips with my family, we always had mbakbaka night. Everyone gathered around the fire as my dad and his friends stirred a big pot, and the anticipation made that first bite unforgettable. This recipe is so nostalgic for me and holds a special place in my heart, and I'm excited to share it with you.

SERVES 6

SPICE BLEND

- 2 teaspoons ground coriander
- 2 teaspoons paprika
- 2 teaspoons salt
- 1 teaspoon ground turmeric
- 1 teaspoon ground ginger
- ½ teaspoon ground allspice
- ½ teaspoon ground cumin
- ½ teaspoon freshly ground black pepper
- ¼ to ½ teaspoon cayenne pepper
- ⅛ teaspoon ground cinnamon

LAMB AND PASTA

- ¼ cup olive oil
- 1½ pounds boneless lamb stew meat, cut into 1-inch cubes
- 1 yellow onion, diced
- 1 tablespoon finely minced garlic
- ⅓ cup tomato paste
- 4 cups low-sodium beef broth
- 1 pound ditalini pasta
- 2 serrano chiles or jalapeños, left whole
- 1 teaspoon dried basil

Make the spice blend: In a small bowl, combine the coriander, paprika, salt, turmeric, ginger, allspice, cumin, black pepper, cayenne, and cinnamon. Mix well.

Cook the lamb and pasta: In a large pot or Dutch oven, heat the olive oil over medium heat. Add the lamb and half of the spice blend and stir to combine. Sauté, stirring occasionally, until the lamb is browned and caramelized, 5 to 7 minutes.

Add the onion and sauté until the onion begins to soften, 7 to 8 minutes.

Add the garlic and tomato paste, give everything a stir, and cook for 2 more minutes to let the tomato paste deepen in flavor. Pour in the beef broth, 2 cups water, and the remaining spice blend. Stir to combine.

Bring the mixture to a simmer. Cover the pot and cook until the lamb becomes tender and easily shreds, 1½ to 2 hours.

Add the pasta, whole serranos or jalapeños, and basil. Stir to combine and cook until the pasta is tender, about 15 minutes.

Transfer to serving bowls or plates and serve hot.

FISH TACO RICE BOWLS

Bowls have to be one of my favorite ways to do dinner. You can take just about any protein, layer it over rice or any carb, add a sauce, and end up with something different yet delicious every time. For this one, I took all the best parts of fish tacos and turned them into a bowl. It starts with the most addictive garlic rice that's good enough to eat on its own. Then comes the fish, pan-fried until golden and crisp. It is way easier than deep-frying but just as tasty. I add a crunchy cabbage slaw for texture and freshness and finish it off with a thick and creamy avocado jalapeño crema. It is everything you want in a taco, just in spoonable form.

SERVES 2 TO 4

SLAW

- 2 tablespoons apple cider vinegar
- 1 tablespoon mayonnaise
- 1 tablespoon sour cream
- 1 teaspoon sugar
- ¼ teaspoon salt
- 2 cups shredded red cabbage
- ¼ red onion, thinly sliced
- 2 green onions, thinly chopped

GARLIC RICE

- 1 tablespoon olive oil
- 1 tablespoon unsalted butter
- 1½ teaspoons minced garlic
- 1 cup jasmine rice, rinsed and drained
- 1 teaspoon salt, or to taste
- 1 small bay leaf

AVOCADO JALAPEÑO CREMA

- 1 avocado
- 1 jalapeño, very finely chopped
- 3 tablespoons sour cream
- 2 tablespoons mayonnaise
- 1 tablespoon fresh lime juice
- ¼ to ½ teaspoon salt, to taste
- ¼ teaspoon freshly ground black pepper

FISH

- 2 tablespoons neutral oil, plus more for pan-frying
- 1 teaspoon chili powder
- ¾ teaspoon salt
- 1 teaspoon Old Bay seasoning
- 1 pound white fish (such as cod, halibut, or mahi mahi), cut into strips ½ inch thick
- 1 cup panko bread crumbs
- Lime wedges, for serving

Make the slaw: In a large bowl, whisk together the vinegar, mayo, sour cream, sugar, and salt until smooth. Add the cabbage, red onion, and green onions directly to the bowl and toss until everything is evenly coated. Cover and set aside in the fridge to marinate while you prep the rest.

Make the garlic rice: In a pot, heat the olive oil and butter over medium heat until hot. Add the garlic and sauté until fragrant, about 1 minute. Add the rice and sauté for 1 to 2 minutes. Add 1⅔ cups water, the salt, and bay leaf and bring to a boil. Cover, reduce the heat to low, and cook for 15 minutes. Turn off the heat and let the rice steam with the lid on for 10 minutes, or until ready to serve. Before serving, remove the lid and fluff with a fork.

Meanwhile, make the avocado jalapeño crema: In a bowl, mash the avocado until smooth. Add the jalapeño, sour cream, mayo, lime juice, salt, and pepper. Mix well until thick, creamy, and combined. Cover and set aside.

Cook the fish: In a small bowl, combine the oil, chili powder, salt, and Old Bay seasoning. Add the fish and toss gently to coat. Place the panko in a separate bowl and press each strip of fish into the panko, coating all sides.

Line a plate with paper towels and have near the stove. In a frying pan, heat just enough oil to cover the bottom of a pan over medium heat. Working in batches to avoid overcrowding, fry the fish until golden and crisp on both sides, 3 to 4 minutes per side depending on the thickness of the fish, using a spatula to very carefully flip at the halfway point—avoid using tongs, as the flaky fish can easily fall apart. Transfer to the paper towels to drain any excess oil.

To serve, add garlic rice to each bowl, followed by a generous pile of slaw. Top with crispy fish, a squeeze of lime, and a big spoonful of avocado crema to enjoy!

SALMON SUSHI-INSPIRED BAKE

What if I told you that you can have all the flavors of a sushi roll without ever learning how to roll one? That's the magic of this salmon sushi bake. The layers are so beautiful. It's just cooked rice, pressed down and topped with a sheet of nori, perfectly baked salmon on top, then the whole thing is finished with creamy mayo, spicy sriracha, and green onions. Less than thirty minutes from start to finish, so it's perfect for those nights when takeout is tempting. It's a true set-it-and-forget-it recipe. The oven does all the work while you unwind, and you still end up with a flavor-packed dinner that feels a little special.

SERVES 4

MARINATED SALMON

- ¼ cup low-sodium soy sauce
- 2 tablespoons brown sugar
- 2 teaspoons toasted sesame oil
- 2 teaspoons minced garlic
- 1 teaspoon paprika
- ¾ teaspoon freshly ground black pepper
- ¾ teaspoon red pepper flakes
- ½ teaspoon salt, or to taste
- 4 skinless salmon fillets (8 ounces each)

ASSEMBLY

- 4 cups cooked sushi rice
- 1 or 2 nori sheets, cut to fit the baking dish
- 2 tablespoons unsalted butter, cut into 4 portions

FOR SERVING

- Kewpie mayo
- Sriracha
- Green onions, thinly sliced, for garnish
- Avocado slices, for topping

Preheat the oven to 400°F. Line a 7 × 10-inch baking dish with parchment paper.

Marinate the salmon: In a bowl, whisk together the soy sauce, brown sugar, sesame oil, garlic, paprika, black pepper, pepper flakes, and salt. Add the salmon and let marinate for 10 to 15 minutes.

Assemble the dish: Add the cooked rice to the baking dish and, using wet hands or a lightly oiled spatula, press it down tightly into an even layer. Place the nori sheet (or sheets) on top of the rice, trimming it to fit. Arrange the salmon fillets side by side on top of the nori. Place ½ tablespoon of butter on top of each fillet.

Bake for 15 minutes, or until the salmon is cooked through and golden on top. Allow to cool for 5 minutes.

To serve: Cut between the fillets into 4 portions, then use a large spatula to lift each portion (with the rice underneath) onto a plate. Drizzle generously with Kewpie mayo and sriracha, then garnish with green onions and avocado slices and enjoy warm!

MEDITERRANEAN SALMON & COUSCOUS

This is a fresh take on a classic one-pot rice and meat dish but reimagined with pearl couscous and salmon. It's loosely inspired by two tomato-based stews: a North African white fish stew my mom still makes regularly and a Greek shrimp stew called shrimp saganaki. While this version swaps shrimp for salmon and adds a nice chew from the couscous, it keeps the heart of both dishes alive with warming spices, tangy feta, and bright tomatoes finished with a squeeze of lemon. In no time at all, you have a vibrant, hearty dish that tastes like it took all day to make.

SERVES 4

SALMON

- 1 tablespoon olive oil
- Grated zest of 1 lemon
- 1 teaspoon smoked paprika
- ¾ teaspoon salt
- ½ teaspoon ground cumin
- ½ teaspoon ground coriander
- ½ teaspoon dried oregano
- ½ teaspoon freshly ground black pepper
- 4 skinless salmon fillets (about 5 ounces each)
- 4 thin lemon slices

COUSCOUS

- 2 tablespoons olive oil
- 2 teaspoons minced garlic
- 3 tablespoons tomato paste
- 1 cup cherry tomatoes, halved
- ½ cup chopped red onion
- ½ teaspoon red pepper flakes
- 1 teaspoon sweet paprika
- 1 teaspoon dried oregano
- 1 to 1½ teaspoons salt, to taste
- ¼ teaspoon freshly ground black pepper
- 1½ cups pearl couscous
- 2 tablespoons unsalted butter

FOR SERVING

- 1 tablespoon finely chopped fresh parsley
- ¼ cup crumbled feta cheese

Cook the salmon: In a small bowl, combine the olive oil, lemon zest, smoked paprika, salt, cumin, coriander, oregano, and black pepper. Rub the mixture evenly over the salmon.

Heat a large sauté pan over medium heat. Add the seasoned fillets and lemon slices to the skillet. Cook until the salmon is cooked through and lightly browned on both sides, 3 to 5 minutes per side. Transfer the salmon and lemon slices to a plate, including any pan juices from cooking.

Cook the couscous: Wipe out and lightly rinse the pan to clean any burnt bits, then return it to medium heat. Add the olive oil and garlic to the pan and sauté until fragrant, about 1 minute. Add the tomato paste and cook, stirring frequently, until it darkens slightly and reduces, 2 to 3 minutes.

Add the cherry tomatoes and red onion to the pan and cook until the tomatoes soften, 3 to 4 more minutes.

Add 2 cups water, the pepper flakes, sweet paprika, oregano, salt, and black pepper and bring to a boil. Add the pearl couscous and give it a quick stir. Reduce the heat to low, cover, and simmer until the couscous is tender and the liquid is absorbed, 12 to 15 minutes.

Uncover and fluff the couscous gently with a spatula or wooden spoon. Stir in the butter until melted and well combined.

To serve: Set the salmon fillets on top of the couscous. Garnish with the cooked lemon slices, chopped parsley, and feta.

MOROCCAN CHICKEN BAKE

This dish is inspired by the Moroccan staple djaj mhammar, roasted chicken with sweet, caramelized onions, tangy preserved lemons, and a generous drizzle of rich olive oil. It's always paired with French fries and bread to soak up all that good sauce.

Traditionally, djaj mhammar is made with a whole chicken, but I wanted to make things easier, so I use drumsticks and thighs instead. No need for stovetop cooking or a pot—everything goes into one pan and straight into the oven.

SERVES 4

- 1 yellow onion, finely chopped
- 5 chicken drumsticks
- 4 bone-in, skin-on chicken thighs
- ¼ cup olive oil
- 1 preserved lemon, rind only, minced
- 2 tablespoons chopped fresh parsley
- 2 tablespoons chopped fresh cilantro
- 1 tablespoon finely minced garlic
- 2 teaspoons paprika
- 2 teaspoons ground ginger
- 1½ teaspoons salt
- 1 teaspoon freshly ground black pepper
- ½ teaspoon ground turmeric
- Pinch of saffron
- 2 tablespoons unsalted butter, melted
- ⅓ cup green olives, to finish
- French fries and/or bread, for serving

Adjust a rack to the lowest position and preheat the oven to 400°F.

Spread the diced onion across the bottom of a 9 × 13-inch baking pan. Pierce the chicken drumsticks and thighs all over with a knife so the marinade can soak deep into every bite, then arrange the chicken pieces right on top of the onions.

In a small bowl, whisk together the olive oil, ¼ cup water, preserved lemon, parsley, cilantro, garlic, paprika, ginger, salt, black pepper, turmeric, and saffron. Pour the marinade all over the chicken and massage it into the skin—don't skip rubbing it under the skin, too.

Place the pan in the oven and roast uncovered for 45 minutes, basting once halfway with the pan juices. Take the pan out and brush the tops of the chicken with the butter. Return to the oven and continue to roast until the skin is beautifully golden brown and crispy, about 5 minutes.

Once it's out, sprinkle with green olives and serve hot with crispy French fries and/or bread on the side.

SHEET-PAN TANDOORI CHICKEN KEFTA KEBABS

This recipe takes inspiration from Persian koobideh—flavorful minced-meat kebabs traditionally wrapped around wide, flat metal skewers and grilled over hot coals—and combines them with the bold flavors of Indian tandoori chicken. No skewers or grill needed here. The spiced meat mixture is pressed into a sheet pan, divided into kebabs, and baked until juicy and tender. It's so much easier than shaping each one on a skewer. Serve with basmati rice, warm naan, and a cooling yogurt dip or fresh cilantro chutney on the side.

SERVES 4

1 pound boneless, skinless chicken thighs
¼ red onion, finely diced
1 jalapeño, seeded and finely diced
¼ cup whole-milk plain yogurt
1 tablespoon ghee
1 tablespoon finely chopped fresh cilantro
2 teaspoons garlic paste or minced fresh garlic
1 teaspoon ginger paste or minced fresh ginger
1½ teaspoons garam masala
1½ teaspoons chili powder
1 teaspoon smoked paprika
1 teaspoon ground coriander
1 teaspoon ground cumin
1 teaspoon ground turmeric
¾ teaspoon salt
¼ to ½ teaspoon cayenne pepper, to taste
3 tablespoons unsalted butter, melted
Juice of ½ lime
Naan (page 212) or steamed basmati rice, for serving

Preheat the oven to 425°F.

Cut the chicken thighs into small chunks. In a food processor or high-powered blender, pulse the chicken until the texture resembles ground meat, but be careful not to overblend into a paste. Scrape down the sides as needed.

In a large bowl, combine the ground chicken, red onion, jalapeño, yogurt, ghee, cilantro, garlic paste, ginger paste, garam masala, chili powder, smoked paprika, coriander, cumin, turmeric, salt, and cayenne. Mix really well until fully combined and sticky.

Lightly grease a 10 × 15-inch nonstick sheet pan. Press the chicken mixture onto the pan into a large, even square, around 8 × 8 inches and about ½ inch thick.

Use a knife to divide the square into 8 long vertical strips, each 1 inch wide, nudging the meat to the side to create a bit of separation between the strips.

Use a chopstick or spatula to press about 8 to 10 indentations crosswise on each kebab. Don't press all the way down—just enough to leave clear ridges on the surface that mimic the look of grilled kefta.

Place the pan in the oven and bake for 6 minutes.

Meanwhile, in a small bowl, mix the melted butter and lime juice.

Take the pan out and baste the kebabs with some of the butter/lime juice mixture using a brush or spoon. Return to the oven and finish baking until fully cooked, 6 to 8 minutes. You'll know they're done when they're firm to the touch, golden on the edges, and no longer pink in the center (you can cut into one to check).

Baste the kebabs with the remaining butter/lime juice mixture and broil for 1 to 3 minutes to get a little char on top. Keep an eye on them so they don't burn!

Serve hot with naan or basmati rice.

HONEY BUFFALO CRISPY CHICKEN WRAPS

I have a confession: I've never been the biggest fan of Buffalo sauce, but since I know so many of you love it, I set out to create a version I could actually get behind. The secret is mixing it with butter and a touch of honey. The combination mellows the heat, cuts the vinegar, and transforms it into a sauce that's creamy with just the right hint of sweetness. The chicken is coated in crushed cornflakes, so it's extra crispy (and gluten-free, if that's something you care about). Made in the air fryer, it's bold, flavorful, and totally changed my mind about Buffalo. I'm officially a fan now!

MAKES 4 WRAPS

CHICKEN

- 3 cups cornflakes
- 2 tablespoons cornstarch
- 2 teaspoons chili powder
- 1 teaspoon paprika
- ½ teaspoon onion powder
- ½ teaspoon garlic powder
- 1 teaspoon salt
- ½ teaspoon freshly ground black pepper
- 1 large egg
- ¼ cup buttermilk
- 1 pound boneless, skinless chicken breasts, cut into bite-size pieces
- Oil spray (for air frying)

Cook the chicken: Preheat an air fryer or an oven to 375°F. If baking in the oven, set a wire rack in a sheet pan.

In a food processor, pulse the cornflakes until coarsely ground.

Set up a dredging station in two wide, shallow bowls: In one bowl, stir together the cornflake crumbs, cornstarch, chili powder, paprika, onion powder, garlic powder, ½ teaspoon of the salt, and ¼ teaspoon of the pepper.

In the other bowl, whisk together the egg, buttermilk, and remaining ½ teaspoon salt and ¼ teaspoon black pepper.

Dip each chicken piece into the egg mixture, coating it well and allowing any excess to drip back into the bowl. Now dredge in the cornflake mixture, pressing gently to adhere.

Spray the air-fryer basket generously with oil and place the coated chicken pieces in the basket. If making it in the oven, arrange the chicken on the wire rack.

Air-fry for 5 to 6 minutes on one side, then flip and cook on the other side until the chicken is golden and crispy, another 5 to 6 minutes. If using the oven, it'll take 2 more minutes on each side.

RECIPE & INGREDIENTS CONTINUE

Meanwhile, make the honey Buffalo sauce: In a small saucepan, combine the Buffalo sauce, butter, honey, pepper flakes, and smoked paprika. Stir over medium heat until the butter is melted and the sauce is well combined. Remove from the heat and set aside.

Assemble the wraps: Transfer the chicken to a bowl and drizzle as much of the Buffalo sauce as you'd like over top.

Warm the flour tortillas slightly, either in the microwave or on a dry skillet, just so they don't tear when stretching and wrapping.

In the center of each tortilla, layer a generous portion (figure ½ to ⅔ cup) of coleslaw and then top with the Buffalo chicken. Fold up the sides of the tortilla and roll tightly to form a wrap.

In a skillet, heat a bit of oil over medium heat. Place the assembled wraps seam-side down in the pan and toast until golden and crispy, 2 to 3 minutes on each side.

Slice each wrap in half before serving.

HONEY BUFFALO SAUCE

- ½ cup Buffalo sauce
- 5 tablespoons unsalted butter
- 2 tablespoons honey
- ½ teaspoon red pepper flakes
- ½ teaspoon smoked paprika

ASSEMBLY

- 4 (10-inch) flour tortillas
- 2 to 3 cups Coleslaw (recipe follows)
- Neutral oil

COLESLAW

In a large bowl, combine the coleslaw mix, green onions, mayo, vinegar, sugar, mustard, and salt. Stir until well combined. Cover and refrigerate for up to 3 days.

MAKES ABOUT 4 CUPS

- 5 cups coleslaw mix (red cabbage, green cabbage, and carrots)
- 2 green onions, thinly sliced
- ¼ cup mayonnaise
- 1 tablespoon apple cider vinegar
- 1 tablespoon sugar
- 1½ teaspoons yellow mustard
- ¼ teaspoon salt

GREEK-INSPIRED CHICKEN GYROS

I've always loved Greek food because it has such fresh, vibrant flavors that make every bite delicious. So, of course, I had to try making gyros at home. Traditionally, gyros are cooked over an open flame on a vertical rotisserie, similar to Arab shawarma or Mexican al pastor. To re-create this at home, you can buy a gyro pan that comes with a skewer that screws into a hole at the base. Don't have one? No problem, I have a hack for you. Just stick two sturdy wooden skewers into a halved onion as a base so it stands up, then thread the chicken onto the skewers. The results are practically identical!

SERVES 4 TO 6

- ½ cup whole-milk plain yogurt
- 2 tablespoons fresh lemon juice
- 2 tablespoons olive oil
- 1 tablespoon minced garlic
- 2 teaspoons salt
- 2 teaspoons ground coriander
- 2 teaspoons dried oregano
- 1 teaspoon ground cumin
- 1 teaspoon smoked paprika
- 1 teaspoon yellow mustard
- ½ teaspoon freshly ground black pepper
- 2½ pounds boneless, skinless chicken thighs
- 1 large onion

FOR SERVING

- Warm pita, homemade (see page 227) or store-bought
- Tzatziki
- Roma tomatoes, thinly sliced
- Cucumbers, diced
- Red onions, thinly sliced
- Crumbled feta cheese

In a large bowl, combine the yogurt, lemon juice, olive oil, garlic, salt, coriander, oregano, cumin, smoked paprika, mustard, and black pepper. Add the chicken thighs and toss to coat. Cover and refrigerate for at least 2 hours, or overnight for deeper flavor.

Remove all but the lower rack from your oven. Preheat the oven to 400°F. If you don't have a gyro pan, soak two wooden skewers in water for 30 minutes.

Prepare the onion by slicing the roots off so there is a wide, flat surface on both sides of the onion.

If using a gyro pan: Thread the onion onto the spit to the bottom. Thread the first chicken thigh onto the spit, piercing it directly through the center. Now skewer your second chicken thigh, but when you push it down to the bottom, rotate it a bit so it's perpendicular to the previous chicken thigh; from above, the two chicken thighs should look like an X, which ensures even cooking. Continue with the remaining chicken thighs, rotating each of them as you go.

If using a sheet pan: Place the onion flat on a sheet pan. Hold the two skewers together, and pierce them into the onion vertically. Thread the marinated chicken thighs onto the skewers using the same X technique outlined above and layering tightly.

For both: Place the prepared pan in the oven and roast until the chicken is fully cooked and reaches an internal temperature of 165°F, 1 hour to 1 hour 15 minutes. Baste the chicken two to three times during cooking to retain moisture. If the chicken starts browning too much, cover it with foil.

Allow the chicken to rest for a few minutes, then remove from the spit or skewers and slice into thin strips. Serve with warm pita, tzatziki, tomatoes, cucumbers, red onions, and feta cheese.

MERGUEZ-SPICED KEFTA SANDWICHES

with Herby Yogurt & Harissa Aioli

Merguez is a North African lamb sausage that's spicy, smoky, and packed with warm spices like cumin and coriander. Since authentic merguez can be hard to find in the US, this sandwich was born as an approachable alternative. By seasoning kefta-style patties with those same bold flavors, you get juicy, flavorful bites that capture the essence of merguez.

SERVES 4

MERGUEZ KEFTA

- 3 tablespoons unsalted butter
- 1½ tablespoons minced garlic
- 1 tablespoon paprika
- 1½ teaspoons ground cumin
- 1½ teaspoons ground coriander
- 1½ pounds ground lamb
- ¼ cup harissa paste
- 1¼ teaspoons salt

HERBY YOGURT SAUCE

- ½ cup whole-milk plain yogurt
- ¾ teaspoon minced garlic
- ¾ teaspoon dried oregano
- ¾ teaspoon dried thyme
- ¾ teaspoon dried parsley
- ½ teaspoon freshly ground black pepper
- Pinch of salt

HARISSA AIOLI

- ½ cup mayonnaise
- 1 tablespoon harissa paste, or more to taste
- 2 teaspoons fresh lemon juice
- ¾ teaspoon smoked paprika

ASSEMBLY

- Neutral oil (optional)
- 1 baguette, cut into 4 pieces
- 1 tomato, thinly sliced
- Salt and freshly ground black pepper
- ½ red onion, thinly sliced
- 8 ounces French fries (see Tip), freshly cooked

Make the kefta: In a small saucepan, melt the butter over medium heat. Add the garlic, paprika, cumin, and coriander and toast, stirring constantly, until fragrant and lightly golden, 1 to 2 minutes. Remove from the heat.

In a large bowl, combine the ground lamb, harissa paste, salt, and the toasted spice/butter mixture. Mix well by hand until fully combined. Cover and refrigerate while preparing the sauces.

Make the herby yogurt sauce: In a small bowl, stir together the yogurt, garlic, oregano, thyme, parsley, black pepper, and salt. Keep chilled.

Make the harissa aioli: In another bowl, whisk together the mayo, harissa, lemon juice, and smoked paprika until smooth. Taste and adjust with more harissa if desired.

Assemble the sandwiches: Divide the lamb mixture into 12 roughly 2-ounce portions. Roll each into a ball, then flatten into small round patties. Heat a skillet or pan over medium-high heat. Lightly grease the pan with neutral oil. Cook the patties until cooked through and golden brown on both sides, about 3 minutes per side. Set aside.

Slice each baguette piece open lengthwise, but don't cut all the way through—leave a hinge. Toast cut-side up under a broiler or cut-side down in a skillet until golden and crisp.

Spread a generous layer of harissa aioli on the bottom side of each toasted baguette. Layer on 3 kefta patties, followed by tomato slices sprinkled with salt and pepper, then red onion. Dollop herby yogurt over the onion, then pile on the cooked French fries. If you like, add more harissa aioli on the top half of the bread. Close the sandwich gently.

Serve hot while the fries are still crisp, the kefta juicy, and the sauces creamy and bold. It's everything you want in one bite.

MORIBYAN'S TIP

I recommend cooking the meat patties and then air-frying or baking the French fries in a conventional oven right before you assemble the sandwiches. That way the fries stay crispy and warm.

CHICKEN SHAWARMA SHEET-PAN BAKE

Here's another quick, thirty-minute weeknight chicken dinner. (You can never have too many, in my opinion.) Whereas the gyros on page 124 are Greek-inspired, this shawarma is inspired by the Levant, with warm spices and a reddish hue. I love to meal-prep it on Sundays and then use the chicken in wraps (just add garlic sauce, pickles, and fries and wrap in pitas), on salads, or over rice. I use red onion as the veggie counterpart, but feel free to add or swap in cauliflower, eggplant, or another vegetable of your choosing. Throw it all on a sheet pan in the oven, roast it, and then you're set for the next few days!

SERVES 4

- ⅓ cup whole-milk plain yogurt
- 2 tablespoons tomato paste
- 2 tablespoons fresh lemon juice
- 2 tablespoons olive oil, plus more for drizzling
- 1 tablespoon minced garlic
- Salt and freshly ground black pepper
- 1½ teaspoons paprika
- 1 teaspoon ground cumin
- 1 teaspoon ground sumac
- 1 teaspoon ground allspice
- 1 teaspoon ground coriander
- ¼ teaspoon ground turmeric
- ⅛ teaspoon ground cardamom
- ⅛ teaspoon ground cinnamon
- 1½ pounds boneless, skinless chicken thighs, cut into strips and chunks
- 1 red onion, cut into 1-inch chunks

In a large bowl, whisk together the yogurt, tomato paste, lemon juice, olive oil, garlic, 1¼ teaspoons salt, ½ teaspoon pepper, and all the spices until smooth and fully combined.

Add the chicken pieces to the bowl and toss until completely coated in the marinade.

You can bake it right away or cover and let it marinate in the fridge for an hour, a few hours, or overnight for deeper flavor.

Preheat the oven to 425°F.

Spread the marinated chicken onto a nonstick sheet pan. Add the red onion directly to the pan around the chicken, then drizzle with olive oil and season with salt and pepper.

Bake for 20 to 25 minutes, until the chicken is cooked through and slightly charred on the edges.

Optional: For extra browning, switch to broil during the last 2 to 3 minutes, keeping a close eye so it doesn't burn.

Let it rest for a few minutes before serving in a wrap, rice bowl, or salad. Store in the fridge for up to 4 days.

CREAMY BUTTER CHICKEN

My brother is obsessed with Indian food, so I made it my mission to master butter chicken at home for him and the rest of my family. What came out of that mission is a dish that's rich, comforting, and full of flavor, with tender pieces of chicken simmered in a creamy tomato-based sauce. The flavors are layered with warm spices, a subtle smokiness, and just the right touch of sweetness to balance the gentle heat. I wanted to make the method as simple as possible. This is truly the easiest butter chicken recipe. No blender, no pureeing, just a handful of ingredients that meld together effortlessly into a dish that tastes like it's been simmering all day.

SERVES 4 WITH LEFTOVERS

CHICKEN

- 1½ pounds boneless, skinless chicken breasts, cubed
- ¼ cup whole-milk plain yogurt
- 1 tablespoon garlic paste or minced fresh garlic
- 2 teaspoons ginger paste or minced fresh ginger
- 1 tablespoon garam masala
- 1 tablespoon ground coriander
- 1½ teaspoons ground turmeric
- 1½ teaspoons ground cumin
- 1 teaspoon cayenne pepper, or to taste
- 1 teaspoon salt
- 1 tablespoon ghee or neutral oil

CURRY

- 2 tablespoons ghee or neutral oil
- 1 teaspoon ginger paste or minced fresh ginger
- 1 teaspoon garlic paste or minced fresh garlic
- 2 teaspoons garam masala
- 1 teaspoon chili powder
- 1 teaspoon paprika
- ½ cup tomato sauce
- ¼ cup tomato paste
- 1 cup heavy cream
- 5 tablespoons unsalted butter
- ½ to ¾ teaspoon salt, to taste
- 1 tablespoon sugar

FOR SERVING

- Steamed basmati rice and/or naan (homemade, page 212, or store-bought)
- Chopped fresh cilantro leaves, for garnish
- Whole-milk plain yogurt, for garnish

Marinate the chicken: In a large bowl, combine the chicken breast cubes, yogurt, garlic paste, ginger paste, garam masala, coriander, turmeric, cumin, cayenne, and salt.

Mix well to coat the chicken evenly. Cover the bowl and refrigerate for at least 30 minutes to marinate (longer for better flavor).

In a large sauté pan, heat the ghee or neutral oil over medium heat. Add the marinated chicken to the pan and cook until golden brown on all sides, 7 to 8 minutes. Remove the chicken from the pan and set it aside.

Make the curry: In the same pan (no need to clean), heat the ghee or neutral oil over medium heat. Add the ginger and garlic pastes and sauté until fragrant, about 1 minute. Stir in the garam masala, chili powder, and paprika, and cook for 30 seconds.

Add the tomato sauce and tomato paste to the pan, mixing well. Cook for 3 to 5 minutes to let the flavors blend and to reduce the acidity.

Pour in the heavy cream and whisk until the sauce becomes smooth and creamy. Add the butter, salt, and sugar and stir to combine until the butter melts completely.

Return the cooked chicken to the pan with the sauce. Stir to coat the chicken in the sauce. Reduce the heat to low and let the chicken simmer in the sauce for 10 minutes to let all the flavors meld together.

To serve: Serve the butter chicken with basmati rice and/or naan, with a garnish of chopped cilantro and a dollop of plain yogurt.

IDRIS'S FAMOUS STUFFED CHICKEN

This Tuscan-inspired stuffed chicken is my husband Idris's signature dish and the very first meal he ever cooked for me. It's since become one of my absolute favorites. The dish comes together so quickly, but it looks and tastes like something you'd order at a fancy restaurant. The chicken is stuffed with creamy ricotta and sun-dried tomatoes, staying juicy on the inside while the outside forms a beautifully golden, flavorful crust. I've kept the recipe exactly as he makes it because it's simply too good to change. If you don't have an air fryer, I've included steps for roasting it in the oven.

SERVES 2 WITH LEFTOVERS

FILLING

- ¾ cup whole-milk ricotta cheese
- ½ cup shredded mozzarella cheese
- ¼ cup grated Parmesan cheese
- ½ cup chopped fresh spinach
- 1 tablespoon chopped fresh basil
- ¼ cup chopped oil-packed sun-dried tomatoes
- 1½ teaspoons oil from sun-dried tomato jar
- 1 teaspoon minced garlic
- ¼ teaspoon red pepper flakes
- ¼ teaspoon salt
- ⅛ teaspoon freshly ground black pepper

CHICKEN

- 3 large boneless, skinless chicken breasts (8 ounces each)
- 2 tablespoons oil from the sun-dried tomato jar
- 1 teaspoon Italian seasoning
- 1 teaspoon paprika
- ¾ teaspoon salt
- ¼ teaspoon freshly ground black pepper

Make the filling: In a medium bowl, combine the ricotta, mozzarella, Parmesan, spinach, basil, sun-dried tomatoes, sun-dried tomato oil, garlic, pepper flakes, salt, and black pepper.

Mix until all ingredients are well combined. Set aside.

Preheat an air fryer to 400°F or preheat the oven to 375°F.

Prepare the chicken: Using a sharp knife, carefully insert the tip of a knife into the thickest part of the side of the chicken breast. Cut a horizontal opening about 3 inches wide, then cut three-quarters of the way through the breast to create a large pocket without cutting all the way through.

Stuff each chicken breast with the filling. Secure the opening with 3 or 4 toothpicks to hold the filling in place.

In a small bowl, mix together the sun-dried tomato oil, Italian seasoning, paprika, salt, and black pepper. Brush this seasoning mixture on both sides of the stuffed chicken breasts.

If air-frying: Place the stuffed chicken breasts in the air fryer. Air-fry for 6 minutes on one side, then carefully flip the chicken and air-fry until a meat thermometer inserted into the thickest part of the chicken reaches 165°F and the chicken is golden brown, 6 to 9 more minutes. Carefully remove the toothpicks from the chicken and serve warm!

If oven-roasting: Place the chicken on a sheet pan and roast until golden, 9 to 12 minutes. Flip over and roast until a meat thermometer inserted into the thickest part of the chicken reads 165°F and the chicken is golden brown, another 9 to 12 minutes. Carefully remove the toothpicks from the chicken and serve warm!

HONEY HARISSA–GLAZED LAMB CHOPS

These lamb chops perfectly balance sweet and spicy thanks to harissa, a classic North African chile paste. The meat turns out unbelievably tender and melts in your mouth. They take just a few minutes to cook and can be enjoyed with the glaze or on their own because the marinade is packed with delicious depth. Lamb chops might sound fancy and a bit intimidating but this recipe makes them totally approachable!

SERVES 4

MARINATED LAMB

- 3 tablespoons olive oil
- 2 teaspoons minced garlic
- 1½ teaspoons salt, or to taste
- 1½ teaspoons ground cumin
- 1½ teaspoons paprika
- 1½ teaspoons dried parsley
- 1 teaspoon dried mint
- ¾ teaspoon freshly ground black pepper
- 12 lamb rib chops (also known as lollipop chops; about 1½ pounds total)

HONEY HARISSA GLAZE

- 4 tablespoons unsalted butter
- 1½ teaspoons minced garlic
- 1½ tablespoons honey
- 1 tablespoon harissa paste
- ¼ teaspoon salt
- ¼ teaspoon freshly ground black pepper
- Squeeze of lemon juice

FOR COOKING

- 1 to 2 tablespoons neutral oil
- 1 to 2 tablespoons unsalted butter

Marinate the lamb: In a large bowl, whisk together the olive oil, garlic, salt, cumin, paprika, parsley, mint, and black pepper. Add the lamb chops and toss to coat. Cover and let them sit for at least 30 minutes at room temperature or refrigerate up to overnight.

Make the honey harissa glaze: In a small saucepan, melt the butter over medium heat. Add the garlic and sauté until fragrant. Stir in the honey, harissa, salt, pepper, and lemon juice. Let it simmer for a minute, then set aside.

Cook the lamb: Heat a skillet over medium-high heat and add ½ to 1 tablespoon of neutral oil. Once hot, cook half of the lamb chops until browned and cooked to your liking (I prefer medium to medium-rare), 2 to 4 minutes per side, depending on thickness. At the last minute, add ½ to 1 tablespoon of butter and use a spoon to baste the chops. Transfer to a plate and set aside. Repeat with the remaining oil, lamb chops, and butter.

Drizzle the honey harissa glaze over the lamb chops and serve immediately.

THE MAIN EVENT

SPATCHCOCKED ROAST CHICKEN
with Gravy

Roasting a whole chicken feels like a grown-up milestone. If this is your first time roasting a whole chicken, I have a feeling it'll come out perfect. By spatchcocking the chicken—removing the backbone and flattening the chicken—it cooks more evenly and gets crispier skin. You can do this yourself or ask a butcher. Once it's roasted, make a quick gravy from the drippings and serve it with roasted potatoes, crispy fries, or the garlic rice from page 110.

SERVES 6

- 1 whole chicken (4 pounds)
- 4 medium carrots, chopped into small rounds
- 4 celery stalks, chopped into small pieces
- 1 yellow onion, quartered and separated
- 10 garlic cloves, left whole
- 4 sprigs thyme
- 1 sprig rosemary
- 2 tablespoons olive oil
- Salt and freshly ground black pepper
- 4 tablespoons unsalted butter, at room temperature

MARINADE

- ¼ cup olive oil
- 2 teaspoons onion powder
- 2 teaspoons garlic powder
- 1½ teaspoons smoked paprika
- 1½ teaspoons sweet paprika
- 1½ teaspoons dried thyme
- 1½ teaspoons dried oregano
- 1½ teaspoons salt, or to taste
- ½ teaspoon freshly ground black pepper
- 2 teaspoons brown sugar
- 2 teaspoons fresh lemon juice
- ¼ teaspoon cayenne pepper
- 1½ teaspoons yellow mustard

GRAVY

- 1½ cups low-sodium chicken broth
- ¼ cup all-purpose flour
- 1 tablespoon unsalted butter
- 1 teaspoon Worcestershire sauce
- ½ teaspoon salt
- ½ teaspoon freshly ground black pepper

To spatchcock the chicken, set the chicken breast-side down on a cutting board and use heavy-duty kitchen shears to cut along both sides of the backbone to remove it. Remove the neck from inside the cavity if it's there. Cut the backbone and neck into 2-inch pieces to roast with the veggies. Flip the chicken over and press firmly on the breastbone to flatten it as much as you can.

Preheat the oven to 400°F.

To a large roasting pan or deep baking tray, add the carrots, celery, onion, garlic, thyme, rosemary, olive oil, ½ teaspoon salt, and ½ teaspoon black pepper. Toss all together with your hands. Scatter the backbone and neck pieces over the veggies. Set up a wire rack on top of the veggies. Add the spatchcocked chicken on top of the wire rack, breast-side up.

Pat the chicken dry with paper towels, then rub the softened butter and 1 teaspoon of salt under the skin.

Make the marinade: In a small bowl, mix the olive oil, onion powder, garlic powder, smoked paprika, sweet paprika, thyme, oregano, salt, black pepper, brown sugar, lemon juice, cayenne, and mustard together until combined. Spread the marinade all over the outside of the chicken.

Place the chicken in the oven and roast until the thickest part of the chicken reads 165°F on an instant-read thermometer, 35 to 45 minutes. Baste the chicken with the pan juices halfway through and again near the end of cooking. Remove the chicken from the oven and let it rest for 10 to 15 minutes before slicing.

Make the gravy: Strain the drippings from the pan, discarding the solid veggies, herbs, and bones. Pour the drippings and chicken broth into a saucepan and bring to a gentle simmer over medium heat. Gradually whisk in the flour until smooth and thickened. Stir in the butter, Worcestershire sauce, salt, and pepper. Adjust the seasoning to taste.

Enjoy the chicken warm with gravy drizzled on top!

JERK CHICKEN SKEWERS
with Coconut Rice & Avocado Mango Salsa

Chicken and rice is my favorite kind of dinner, so I'm always looking for new ways to make it exciting. This version takes inspiration from Caribbean jerk chicken, which is traditionally marinated with Scotch bonnet peppers, allspice, thyme, and citrus, then cooked low and slow over smoky heat. Here, those same flavors get a faster, more weeknight-friendly twist with juicy chicken skewers cooked in the air fryer. And if that wasn't enough, we're pairing it with fluffy coconut rice that's lightly sweet and fragrant, and a refreshing mango, avocado, and jalapeño salsa that ties it all together.

SERVES 3 OR 4

JERK CHICKEN

- 2 tablespoons avocado oil
- 1 to 2 habaneros or Scotch bonnet peppers, to taste, seeded
- ¼ red onion
- 3 garlic cloves, left whole
- 2 green onions
- 1 teaspoon ground allspice
- ¼ cup soy sauce
- 1-inch piece fresh ginger
- 2 teaspoons fresh thyme
- Grated zest and juice of ½ orange
- Grated zest and juice of ½ lime
- 2 tablespoons brown sugar
- 1 tablespoon apple cider vinegar
- 1 teaspoon salt
- ¼ teaspoon freshly ground black pepper
- ¼ teaspoon ground cinnamon
- ¼ teaspoon ground nutmeg
- 1½ pounds boneless, skinless chicken thighs, cut into chunks

AVOCADO MANGO SALSA

- 1 mango, diced
- 1 avocado, diced
- ¼ red onion, finely chopped
- 1 jalapeño, seeded and finely chopped
- Juice of ½ lime
- 2 tablespoons chopped fresh cilantro
- Salt

COCONUT RICE

- 1 tablespoon unsalted butter
- 1 tablespoon minced garlic
- 1 (13.5-ounce) can full-fat coconut milk
- 2 tablespoons granulated sugar
- 2 teaspoons salt
- 2 cups jasmine rice, rinsed well

Marinate the jerk chicken: In a blender, combine the avocado oil, habaneros, red onion, garlic cloves, green onions, allspice, soy sauce, ginger, thyme, orange zest, orange juice, lime zest, lime juice, brown sugar, vinegar, salt, black pepper, cinnamon, and nutmeg. Blend until smooth. Reserve 3 tablespoons of the marinade in a small bowl.

Place the chicken thighs in a large bowl and pour the remaining marinade over the top. Toss to coat evenly, cover, and marinate for at least 30 minutes, but ideally 2 hours or up to overnight for maximum flavor.

Soak 5 wooden skewers in water for 30 minutes.

Thread the marinated chicken onto the soaked skewers. Set aside.

Make the avocado mango salsa: In a medium bowl, combine the mango, avocado, red onion, jalapeño, lime juice, and cilantro. Season with salt to taste. Gently toss to combine, ensuring the avocado remains chunky. Adjust seasoning as needed. Cover and refrigerate while you make the rest.

Make the coconut rice: In a medium pot, melt the butter over medium heat. Add the garlic and sauté until fragrant, about 1 minute. Pour in the coconut milk, 1⅓ cups water, granulated sugar, and salt. Mix well and bring to a boil.

Add the jasmine rice, bring back to a boil, then reduce the heat to low. Cover and simmer for 15 minutes. Turn off the heat but keep the pot covered for 10 more minutes.

While the rice is resting, preheat an air fryer to 400°F. Place the skewers in the air fryer basket, but make sure not to overcrowd it (depending on the size of your air fryer, you may need to do this in batches). Air-fry until the chicken is cooked through and slightly charred, 13 to 15 minutes, turning halfway through and basting with the reserved marinade.

To serve, fluff the coconut rice with a fork. Plate the jerk chicken skewers over a bed of coconut rice, and top with the avocado mango salsa. Enjoy!

CHICKEN ENCHILADAS

This was the first dish I ever made for my now-husband, and it must have been good because we've been together ever since. The tortillas are rolled up with tender shredded chicken, smothered in a rich, tangy enchilada sauce, and baked under a blanket of bubbly, golden cheese that crisps around the edges. Every bite is warm and comforting with just the right balance of smoky spice and melty goodness. On days when I have less time, I shred a rotisserie chicken instead of poaching the chicken myself.

SERVES 4

POACHED CHICKEN

- 2 chicken bouillon cubes
- 2 bay leaves
- 2 large boneless, skinless chicken breasts (about 1½ pounds total)

CHICKEN FILLING

- 1 tablespoon avocado oil
- ½ large red bell pepper, diced
- ½ large green bell pepper, diced
- 2 teaspoons minced garlic
- ¼ cup tomato sauce
- 3 tablespoons mild fire-roasted chopped chiles
- 1 tablespoon sauce from canned chipotles in adobo
- 1½ teaspoons Worcestershire sauce
- 2 teaspoons chili powder
- 1 teaspoon ground coriander
- 1 teaspoon ground cumin
- 1 teaspoon dried oregano
- 1 teaspoon salt
- ½ teaspoon onion powder

ASSEMBLY

- 8 medium (about 8-inch) flour tortillas
- 2 cups mild red enchilada sauce
- ⅓ cup sour cream
- 1½ to 2 cups shredded Mexican cheese blend, or as desired

FOR SERVING (OPTIONAL)

- Fresh cilantro
- Diced onions
- Sour cream
- Guacamole
- Hot sauce

Preheat the oven to 350°F. Grease a 9 × 13-inch baking dish.

Poach the chicken: In a large pot, bring 8 cups water to a boil with the bouillon cubes and bay leaves. Add the chicken breasts and boil until cooked through, 15 to 20 minutes, depending on thickness. Remove the chicken, let it cool, then shred with two forks or your hands.

Make the chicken filling: In a large skillet, heat the avocado oil over medium heat. Add the red and green bell peppers and sauté until softened, 5 to 6 minutes. Stir in the garlic and cook for 1 minute more.

Add the shredded chicken and stir in the tomato sauce, chopped chiles, adobo sauce, Worcestershire sauce, chili powder, coriander, cumin, oregano, salt, and onion powder. Mix until the chicken is well-coated and heated through.

Assemble and bake the enchiladas: Divide the chicken filling among the tortillas, then roll each one and place it, seam-side down, in the prepared pan.

In a bowl, mix the enchilada sauce and sour cream until combined. Pour the sauce over the assembled enchiladas, ensuring they are fully covered. Sprinkle the shredded cheese on top of the enchiladas.

Bake until the cheese is melted and bubbling, 20 to 25 minutes. For a golden finish, broil for an additional 2 to 3 minutes, watching closely to prevent burning.

Let the enchiladas cool slightly before serving. Enjoy your homemade chicken enchiladas with your favorite toppings, if desired, such as fresh cilantro, diced onions, sour cream, a dollop of guacamole, and hot sauce!

CHICKEN BIRYANI

This isn't a super-traditional biryani—the spice level is toned down a bit, and I like to use boneless chicken to keep it easy. But it's still so flavorful. The rice and chicken are layered with warm spices, and the chicken turns out tender and juicy. The subtle heat is balanced with fresh herbs like cilantro and mint. The fried onions add sweetness, while a touch of saffron brings a floral aroma that ties everything together for the most epic bite.

Marinate the chicken: In a bowl, combine the yogurt, biryani masala, lemon juice, salt, paprika, coriander, cayenne, and turmeric. Add the chicken and toss until fully coated. Cover and set aside at room temp to marinate.

Fry the onions: Line a plate with paper towels and have near the stove. In a large pot, heat the oil over medium heat. Once hot, add the onions and fry until deeply golden and crisp, 10 to 12 minutes, stirring often. Remove with a slotted spoon and drain on paper towels.

Make the rice: Drain the rice well. In a large pot, bring 8 cups water and the salt to a boil. Add the whole spices—cinnamon stick, cardamom pods, cloves, bay leaves, cumin seeds, star anise, and peppercorns. You can tie them in a spice bag for easy removal, or leave them loose if you don't mind picking them out later. Once boiling, add the soaked and drained rice. Cook for 5 minutes—just until it's 75 percent done (the grains should still have a bit of bite). Drain and set aside.

Assemble the biryani: In a large heavy-bottomed pot or Dutch oven, melt 2 tablespoons of the ghee over medium heat. Add the tomato paste, garlic paste, and ginger paste and sauté until fragrant and the tomato paste deepens in color, 2 to 3 minutes. Add the marinated chicken and cook until browned and just cooked through, 6 to 7 minutes.

Top the chicken with the green chiles, half of the fried onions, half of the chopped mint, and half of the cilantro. Spread the parboiled rice on top in an even layer. Sprinkle on the remaining fried onions and the remaining mint and cilantro. Season with salt. Pour the saffron milk over the rice and drizzle on the remaining 1 tablespoon ghee. Use a chopstick or the handle of a wooden spoon to poke a few holes in the biryani, all the way down to the bottom, and sprinkle over the biryani masala.

Seal the pot tightly with foil first to trap the steam, then place a tight-fitting lid on top. Cook over low heat on the stovetop for 25 minutes. Turn off the heat and let it sit, still covered, for 10 more minutes.

To plate, scoop all the way from the bottom and gently transfer to a large serving platter. This way, you get those beautiful colors: tender chicken and rice that's yellow, orange, and white throughout.

SERVES 6

MARINATED CHICKEN

- ½ cup whole-milk plain yogurt
- 2 tablespoons biryani masala
- 1 tablespoon fresh lemon juice
- 1½ teaspoons salt
- 1 teaspoon paprika
- 1 teaspoon ground coriander
- ½ to 1 teaspoon cayenne pepper, to taste
- ½ teaspoon ground turmeric
- 1½ pounds boneless, skinless chicken thighs, cut into chunks

FRIED ONIONS

- 1 cup neutral oil, for frying
- 1 red onion, thinly sliced

RICE

- 2 cups basmati rice, rinsed in cold water until it runs mostly clear (3 or 4 times), then soaked for 30 minutes
- 2 tablespoons salt
- 1 cinnamon stick
- 6 green cardamom pods
- 6 whole cloves
- 3 bay leaves
- ½ teaspoon cumin seeds
- 1 star anise
- ½ teaspoon black peppercorns

ASSEMBLY

- 3 tablespoons ghee
- 2 tablespoons tomato paste
- 1 tablespoon garlic paste
- 1 tablespoon ginger paste
- 2 green chiles (left whole for less spicy, chopped for very spicy)
- ¼ cup chopped fresh mint
- ¼ cup chopped fresh cilantro
- Saffron milk: ¼ teaspoon saffron threads soaked in 2 tablespoons milk
- 1 teaspoon biryani masala

CREAMY TUSCAN CHICKEN PASTA

This pasta is my twist on the Internet-famous Marry Me Chicken, but instead of chicken breasts, you get golden, flavorful chicken sausage crumbles tossed into a creamy sun-dried tomato sauce. It's rich from the cream and Parmesan, a little tangy from the tomatoes, and finished with fresh herbs to brighten everything up. Sometimes I even take this recipe and roll the chicken into meatballs, then cook spaghetti as my pasta of choice for a fun take on "spaghetti and meatballs"—except the meatballs are chicken and the sauce is that creamy Tuscan-style we all love.

SERVES 4

CHICKEN "SAUSAGE"

- 1 tablespoon olive oil
- 1 pound ground chicken
- 1½ teaspoons Italian seasoning
- 1½ teaspoons paprika
- 1 teaspoon red pepper flakes
- 1 teaspoon salt
- ½ teaspoon onion powder
- ½ teaspoon garlic powder

PASTA AND SAUCE

- 1 tablespoon olive oil
- 1 tablespoon unsalted butter
- ¼ large red onion, diced
- 1 tablespoon minced garlic
- 3 tablespoons tomato paste
- ½ cup sun-dried tomatoes, blended into a paste
- 1 cup heavy cream
- 1 cup chicken broth
- 2 tablespoons cream cheese, at room temperature
- ½ teaspoon dried oregano
- ½ teaspoon red pepper flakes, plus more for serving
- ½ teaspoon freshly ground black pepper
- Salt
- ½ cup grated Parmesan cheese, plus more for serving
- 12 ounces pasta of choice
- 1 tablespoon chopped fresh basil
- 1 tablespoon chopped fresh parsley

Cook the chicken "sausage": In a large sauté pan, heat the olive oil over medium heat. Add the ground chicken, Italian seasoning, paprika, pepper flakes, salt, onion powder, and garlic powder. Cook, breaking it up with a wooden spoon, until browned and cooked through, 7 to 8 minutes. Transfer to a plate and set aside.

Make the pasta sauce: In the same pan, heat the oil and butter over medium heat. Add the red onion and sauté until softened, 2 to 3 minutes. Add the garlic and sauté for 30 more seconds.

Add the tomato paste and sun-dried tomato paste and cook, stirring occasionally, until darkened slightly, about 2 minutes. Add the heavy cream, chicken broth, and cream cheese and whisk together until smooth.

Season with the oregano, pepper flakes, black pepper, and a pinch of salt. Stir in the Parmesan, then reduce the heat to low and let the sauce simmer for 2 to 3 minutes for the flavors to come together.

Meanwhile, in a large pot of salted boiling water, cook the pasta according to package directions.

Return the cooked chicken sausage mixture to the sauce, tossing to coat. Finally, add the chopped basil and parsley to the sauce and give it a quick stir. Taste and add salt as needed.

Drain the pasta, add to the sauce, and toss, letting it simmer all together for 2 to 3 minutes so the pasta finishes cooking and the sauce clings perfectly.

Serve hot, with more Parmesan and red pepper flakes on top.

CHICKEN PARMESAN PASTA BAKE

Here, I turn classic chicken Parmesan into a pasta bake that feeds a crowd and boasts the flavors we all love: juicy chicken cutlets nestled on top of saucy pasta, finished with layers of molten mozzarella, crispy golden edges, and plenty of bubbling sauce.

SERVES 4

CRISPY CHICKEN

- 2 large boneless, skinless chicken breasts (about 8 ounces each)
- Salt
- ½ cup all-purpose flour
- Freshly ground black pepper
- 2 large eggs
- 2½ teaspoons Italian seasoning
- ¼ cup plus 2 tablespoons grated Parmesan cheese
- 1 cup fine dried bread crumbs
- 1 teaspoon dried oregano
- 1 teaspoon dried parsley
- Neutral oil, for frying

PASTA AND SAUCE

- Salt
- 12 ounces penne
- 1 tablespoon olive oil
- 1 tablespoon unsalted butter
- 1 tablespoon minced garlic
- 5 cups marinara sauce
- ½ cup heavy cream
- ½ to 1 teaspoon red pepper flakes, to taste
- 1 tablespoon chopped fresh parsley
- 1 tablespoon chopped fresh basil
- ¼ cup shredded Parmesan cheese

ASSEMBLY

- 5 ounces mozzarella cheese, shredded or slices
- ¼ cup grated Parmesan cheese

Make the crispy chicken: Cut each chicken breast in half horizontally into 2 thinner cutlets. Working one at a time, cover the cutlets with plastic wrap and pound them out to an even thinness. Lightly salt both sides.

Set up a dredging station in three wide, shallow bowls: In one bowl, mix the flour with ½ teaspoon salt and ½ teaspoon black pepper. In a second bowl, mix together the eggs, 1 teaspoon of the Italian seasoning, 2 tablespoons of the Parmesan, ½ teaspoon salt, and ¼ teaspoon black pepper. In the third bowl, mix together the bread crumbs, remaining ¼ cup Parmesan, remaining 1½ teaspoons Italian seasoning, the oregano, dried parsley, ½ teaspoon salt, and ½ teaspoon pepper.

With one hand for the dry ingredients and one for the wet, coat each chicken cutlet in the flour mixture, then dip into the egg mixture, and finally coat in the bread crumb mixture, pressing gently to adhere.

Set a wire rack in a sheet pan and have near the stove. In a large skillet, heat about ½ inch of oil over medium heat until it reaches 325°F. Fry each cutlet until golden brown and crispy and the internal temperature reaches 165°F, 3 to 4 minutes per side. Transfer to the wire rack to stay crispy.

Preheat the oven to 375°F.

Make the pasta and sauce: In a pot of boiling salted water, cook the penne according to package directions.

Meanwhile, in a large pot, heat the olive oil and butter over medium heat. Add the garlic and sauté until golden, about 1 minute. Stir in the marinara, heavy cream, and pepper flakes and simmer until fragrant, 5 to 6 minutes. Stir in the parsley, basil, and Parmesan and remove from the heat.

Measure out 1 cup of the sauce and set aside. Drain the pasta and add to the rest of the sauce, mixing well to coat.

Assemble and bake: Transfer the sauced pasta to an 8 × 11-inch baking dish. Arrange the cutlets on top. Spoon ¼ cup of the reserved sauce over each cutlet. Add the mozzarella, then finish with a sprinkle of Parmesan.

Bake uncovered for 10 minutes, then broil until golden and bubbling on top, 2 to 4 minutes. Serve hot!

HAWAIIAN-INSPIRED GARLIC SHRIMP

with Mac Salad

This famous Hawaiian dish features crispy, garlic butter–drenched shrimp that will leave you licking the plate. The key is the garlic—it may seem like a lot, but don't let it intimidate you. When sautéed in a generous amount of butter, the garlic turns golden, caramelized, and almost sweet in flavor. Traditionally, the shrimp are coated in mochiko (sweet rice flour), which gives it that unique, crispy texture. Since mochiko can be hard to find, I've swapped it for a simple mix of all-purpose flour and cornstarch to get the same satisfying crunch.

SERVES 4

MACARONI SALAD

- Salt
- 1 pound elbow macaroni
- 2 cups mayonnaise
- ½ cup whole milk
- 1 tablespoon yellow mustard
- 3 tablespoons apple cider vinegar
- 2 tablespoons sugar
- ½ teaspoon freshly ground black pepper
- 1 cup shredded carrots

SHRIMP

- 1½ tablespoons all-purpose flour (see Tips)
- 1½ tablespoons cornstarch (see Tips)
- 2 teaspoons paprika
- 1 teaspoon salt
- ¼ teaspoon freshly ground black pepper
- ¼ to ½ teaspoon cayenne pepper or red pepper flakes, to taste
- 1 pound large shrimp, peeled, deveined, and tail on
- 5 tablespoons unsalted butter
- ¼ cup finely minced garlic
- 2 tablespoons olive oil

Lemon wedges, for serving

Make the macaroni salad: In a large pot of salted boiling water, cook the macaroni according to package directions. Drain and rinse.

In a small bowl, whisk together the mayonnaise, milk, mustard, vinegar, sugar, 1 teaspoon salt, and the black pepper until smooth.

In a large bowl, combine the cooked macaroni, shredded carrots, and half the mayonnaise sauce, then toss until evenly coated. Cover and refrigerate the salad and the remaining mayonnaise sauce separately.

Cook the shrimp: In a medium bowl, whisk together the all-purpose flour, cornstarch, paprika, salt, black pepper, and cayenne until evenly combined. Add the shrimp and toss together so each shrimp is fully coated.

In a large sauté pan, melt the butter over medium-low heat. Add the garlic and cook until golden brown, toasted, and fragrant, about 3 minutes. Transfer the garlic and butter to a bowl and set aside.

In the same pan (no need to clean!), heat the olive oil over medium-high heat until hot. Working in batches to avoid overcrowding, cook the shrimp until crispy and golden, 2 to 3 minutes per side.

Once all the shrimp are cooked, return the garlic and butter to the pan and toss everything together.

Right before serving, toss the macaroni salad with the remaining mayonnaise sauce. Serve the shrimp immediately alongside the macaroni salad (see Tips), with lemon wedges for squeezing. Enjoy!

MORIBYAN'S TIPS

You can use 3 tablespoons of mochiko (sweet rice flour) instead of all-purpose flour and cornstarch for a more authentic crispy texture.

Feel free to also serve this with white rice instead of macaroni salad—or serve it with both!

LOADED EGGPLANT
with Beef, Garlic Yogurt & Chile Butter

I like to think of this as a Middle Eastern twist on the classic American baked potato. But instead of a baked potato, you get rich, creamy roasted eggplant piled high with spiced ground beef, smoky chile butter, and a tangy dill-and-garlic yogurt. It's inspired by Turkish manti and Afghan mantu. This dish takes those same bold flavors and elevates eggplant to a whole new level.

SERVES 4

EGGPLANT

- 2 large eggplants, stem ends trimmed
- ½ teaspoon salt
- 1 tablespoon olive oil
- ¼ teaspoon freshly ground black pepper

YOGURT SAUCE

- 1 cup whole-milk plain yogurt
- 1 tablespoon olive oil
- 1 teaspoon grated lemon zest
- 1 teaspoon chopped fresh dill
- ¼ teaspoon freshly ground black pepper
- ¼ teaspoon salt

GROUND BEEF

- 1 tablespoon olive oil
- ½ yellow onion, diced
- 1 pound ground beef (90/10 or 85/15)
- 1 teaspoon ground cumin
- 1 teaspoon ground coriander
- 1 teaspoon paprika
- ¾ teaspoon salt
- ½ teaspoon ground allspice
- ½ teaspoon ground ginger
- ¼ teaspoon freshly ground black pepper
- ¼ cup tomato sauce

CHILE BUTTER

- 5 tablespoons unsalted butter
- 2 teaspoons minced garlic
- 1 teaspoon Aleppo pepper
- 1 teaspoon paprika
- 1 teaspoon red pepper flakes
- ¼ teaspoon salt

Roast the eggplant: Preheat the oven to 350°F. Line a large baking sheet with parchment.

Cut the eggplant in half lengthwise. Score the flesh in a crisscross pattern, being careful not to cut through the skin. Sprinkle ¼ teaspoon of the salt over all the cut sides, then place them cut-side down on a wire rack to remove any excess moisture. Let sit for 30 minutes, patting dry with a paper towel every 10 minutes.

In a small bowl, mix the olive oil, pepper, and remaining ¼ teaspoon salt. Drizzle the flesh side of the eggplant with the olive oil mixture, letting it seep into the cuts.

Transfer cut-side up to the prepared baking sheet and roast until the flesh is golden and tender, 40 to 45 minutes.

Meanwhile, make the yogurt sauce: In a small bowl, whisk together the yogurt, olive oil, lemon zest, dill, black pepper, and salt. Set aside.

Cook the ground beef: In a large sauté pan, heat the olive oil over medium-high heat. Add the onion and sauté until softened and golden, 8 to 10 minutes.

Add the ground beef, using a spoon or spatula to break it apart as it cooks. Season with the cumin, coriander, paprika, salt, allspice, ginger, and black pepper. Cook until the beef is browned, 8 to 9 minutes.

Pour in the tomato sauce, mix well, and cook down for 1 to 2 minutes.

Make the chile butter: In a small pan, melt the butter over low heat. Add the garlic, Aleppo pepper, paprika, red pepper flakes, and salt. Stir and let sizzle for 2 to 3 minutes until fragrant.

Place the roasted eggplant halves, flesh-side up, on a serving plate. Spoon the ground beef mixture over the eggplant. Add a generous dollop of the yogurt sauce across the top and drizzle with the warm chile butter.

Serve immediately and enjoy!

CHILI CHEESE LOADED POTATO BOWLS

A bowl of chili is good, but chili piled over crispy roasted potatoes and smothered in thick, creamy chili? That's next level. I always felt like chili was missing a carb to make it truly complete, and these loaded potato bowls deliver just that. I love this in the colder months because it's so hearty with ground beef, beans, and potatoes all in one bowl.

SERVES 4

ROASTED POTATOES

- 2 pounds potatoes, cut into ¾-inch pieces
- 1 teaspoon salt
- ¼ teaspoon freshly ground black pepper
- 2 tablespoons neutral oil
- 1½ teaspoons cornstarch

CHILI

- 2 tablespoons neutral oil
- 1 red bell pepper, diced small
- 1 jalapeño, seeded and diced small
- ½ yellow onion, diced small
- 1 tablespoon minced garlic
- 1 pound ground beef (90/10)
- 1 tablespoon chili powder
- 1 teaspoon smoked paprika
- 1 teaspoon ground cumin
- 1 teaspoon ground coriander
- 1 teaspoon salt, or to taste
- ¾ teaspoon dried oregano
- ¼ teaspoon freshly ground black pepper
- ¼ teaspoon onion powder
- Pinch of cayenne pepper, or to taste
- 1½ teaspoons light brown sugar
- 1 cup canned fire-roasted diced tomatoes
- ½ cup tomato sauce
- 1 teaspoon Worcestershire sauce
- 1 cup beans (pinto, kidney, black, or a mix), rinsed and drained

FOR SERVING

- Shredded cheddar cheese
- Sour cream
- Sliced jalapeños
- Thinly sliced green onions
- Finely chopped fresh cilantro

Roast the potatoes: Preheat the oven to 425°F.

In a large bowl, combine the potatoes, salt, pepper, oil, and cornstarch. Toss until evenly coated. Spread the potatoes out in a single layer on a nonstick baking sheet and transfer to the oven.

Roast, flipping halfway through, until golden and crispy and fully cooked through, 35 to 40 minutes.

Meanwhile, make the chili: In a large skillet or sauté pan, heat the oil over medium heat. Add the bell pepper, jalapeño, and onion and sauté until softened, 5 to 6 minutes. Add the garlic and cook for another minute.

Add the ground beef to the pan and cook until browned, breaking it apart with a spatula, 6 to 8 minutes.

Stir in the chili powder, smoked paprika, cumin, coriander, salt, oregano, black pepper, onion powder, cayenne, and brown sugar. Mix until the meat is fully coated in the spices. Pour in the fire-roasted diced tomatoes, tomato sauce, and Worcestershire sauce. Stir well, then add the beans. Reduce the heat to low and simmer for 10 to 15 minutes to thicken.

To serve: Spoon the roasted potatoes into bowls and top with a generous scoop of chili. Add shredded cheddar, a few dollops of sour cream, sliced jalapeños, green onions, and a sprinkle of chopped cilantro to finish.

MAMA REEM'S FILFIL MAHSHEE

(Libyan Stuffed Peppers)

This is my favorite dish my mother-in-law, Reem, makes. *Filfil mahshee* translates to "stuffed peppers" in Arabic, and while every Middle Eastern country makes it a little differently, this is how we make it in Libya. Sweet bell peppers are filled with a fragrant mixture of rice, meat, and warm spices, then slowly cooked in a tangy tomato sauce until the peppers are tender and the filling soaks up all the flavor. The sweetness of the peppers balances the savory, spiced meat and the bright acidity of the sauce. You can also stuff other vegetables like onions and grape leaves. The final presentation is stunning, yet the recipe is surprisingly straightforward. It's also a perfect dish for entertaining, since you can prep it in advance and pop it in the oven to cook away when your guests arrive.

SERVES 6

- 12 small or 10 medium bell peppers
- 1 beefsteak tomato, cored
- 6 green onions (1 small bunch), green parts only
- 1 small bunch cilantro, stems removed
- 1 small bunch parsley, stems removed
- 1 small bunch dill
- 1 pound lamb stew meat, chopped very fine (see Tip, page 160), ground lamb, or ground beef
- 1 cup long-grain rice, rinsed well
- 3 tablespoons tomato paste
- 3 tablespoons olive oil
- 2 teaspoons salt
- 2 teaspoons paprika
- 1 teaspoon ground coriander
- 1 teaspoon ground ginger
- ½ teaspoon freshly ground black pepper
- ½ teaspoon ground turmeric
- ¼ teaspoon cayenne pepper
- Pinch of ground cardamom
- Pinch of ground cinnamon

Take a sharp knife and carefully cut a circle around the top of each bell pepper, keeping the stem and top intact like a little lid. Remove the seed core and inner ribs but save the tops to use later as covers. You can cook the peppers on the stovetop or in the oven. For the stovetop, place the cleaned peppers upright and snugly in a large, deep pot or wide pan with a lid. If baking in the oven, use a large deep metal or ceramic baking dish.

Finely chop the tomato, green onions, cilantro, parsley, and dill by hand until everything is chopped very small.

In a large bowl, combine the chopped herbs and tomato, the meat, rice, tomato paste, olive oil, salt, paprika, coriander, ginger, black pepper, turmeric, cayenne, cardamom, and cinnamon. Mix thoroughly until the ingredients are evenly combined.

Spoon the filling into each prepared pepper, filling them almost to the top but without packing it in too tightly (the rice needs room to expand as it cooks). Place the saved pepper tops back on like little covers.

RECIPE & INGREDIENTS CONTINUE

Make the cooking liquid: In a bowl, whisk together the tomato paste, hot beef broth, olive oil, garlic, black pepper, salt, turmeric, and cayenne until smooth.

Pour 3 to 4 tablespoons of the cooking liquid into each pepper. Then pour any remaining liquid into the bottom of the pan, pot, or baking dish around the peppers.

To cook on the stovetop: Cover the pan or pot very tightly with foil, then press the lid on top and seal it all around to lock in the steam. Set the pan or pot over medium heat and let it come to a gentle simmer. Once bubbling, reduce the heat to medium-low and let it cook until the rice is tender and the peppers are soft, 1 hour to 1 hour 15 minutes.

To cook in the oven: Preheat the oven to 400°F. Wrap the dish tightly with foil all around to make sure no steam escapes. If your dish has a lid, even better. I like to put a heavy baking sheet on top to help everything stay sealed tightly. Bake the covered dish until the peppers are tender and the rice is fully cooked inside, 1 hour to 1 hour 15 minutes. Once the rice is tender, uncover and bake for 10 to 15 more minutes just to get some caramelization on top.

For both: Let the peppers rest for 10 minutes before serving. For the best presentation, gently remove the peppers from the cooking liquid so they don't get soggy. Save the liquid—it's full of flavor—and drizzle a little over each plate when serving.

MORIBYAN'S TIP

Chopped lamb stew meat is the most traditional choice here, but you can substitute ground lamb or ground beef, if you'd like. This saves a lot of time as chopping the lamb that tiny gets tedious.

COOKING LIQUID

- ½ cup tomato paste
- 2 cups beef broth, heated
- 2 tablespoons olive oil
- 2 teaspoons minced garlic
- 1 teaspoon freshly ground black pepper
- ½ teaspoon salt
- ½ teaspoon ground turmeric
- ¼ teaspoon cayenne pepper

STEAK FRITES
with Peppercorn Sauce

My husband and I can't resist steak frites when it's on a restaurant menu. No matter what city we're in, we're always on the lookout for a great steak frites spot to satisfy that craving. The best versions are sublime: hot, crispy fries and perfectly cooked steak smothered in a creamy, peppery sauce. This recipe is just as good as what you'll find at most restaurants and way more affordable. The frites are double-fried for extra crispiness, and the steak gets that perfect sear before being finished with a dreamy pepper sauce.

SERVES 2

FRIES

- 1 pound russet potatoes, rinsed and peeled
- Salt
- 1 tablespoon cornstarch
- Vegetable oil, for frying

STEAK

- 1-pound boneless rib-eye steak (1¼ inches thick), at room temperature
- ½ teaspoon salt
- ¼ teaspoon freshly ground black pepper
- 1 tablespoon neutral oil
- 1 tablespoon unsalted butter

Make the fries: Start by cutting each potato lengthwise into rectangular slices, about ¼ inch thick. Stack these slices, then cut them lengthwise again to create long, thin fries. You can adjust the thickness based on your preference.

Transfer the potatoes to a bowl filled with ice water and let them soak for 30 minutes.

Drain and rinse the potatoes 2 or 3 times, shaking them around to remove excess starch.

Bring a pot of salted water to a boil. Add the potatoes and parboil until slightly tender but not falling apart, 4 to 5 minutes.

Drain and pat the potatoes completely dry. Transfer to a tray or large bowl and toss with cornstarch to coat evenly.

Set a wire rack in a sheet pan and have near the stove. Pour 2 to 3 inches of oil into a deep, heavy-bottomed pan and heat over medium-low heat until it reaches 275° to 300°F on a deep-fry thermometer.

Working in batches, fry the potatoes until they hold their shape but are just slightly golden on the edges, 3 to 5 minutes. Drain on a wire rack while you prepare the steak.

Cook the steak: Pat the steak dry with paper towels. Season both sides with the salt and black pepper.

Heat a cast-iron skillet over medium-high heat for 3 to 4 minutes, or until it's smoking hot. Add the neutral oil to the pan.

Using tongs to hold the steak, sear the fat cap for 1 to 2 minutes to render the fat and create a crispy edge.

RECIPE & INGREDIENTS CONTINUE

Lay the steak flat in the skillet and sear on the first side without moving it, allowing a nice crust to form, 2 to 3 minutes. Flip the steak and sear the second side to achieve a golden, crispy crust, another 2 to 3 minutes.

Reduce the heat to medium-low. Add the butter to the skillet. As the butter melts, tilt the pan slightly and use a spoon to baste the steak with the butter. Do this for 1 to 2 minutes, spooning the melted butter over the steak to infuse it with flavor. Flip the steak and baste the other side for 1 to 2 minutes, or until you've achieved your preferred doneness (I like medium-rare, so I pull the steak at 130°F).

Remove the steak from the skillet and let it rest for 5 to 10 minutes. The steak will continue to cook slightly from residual heat. Hold on to the skillet for making the peppercorn sauce.

Fry the potatoes again and make the peppercorn sauce: Here is where it helps to have two people, since ideally you would make the peppercorn sauce and also do the second fry on the potatoes at the same time.

Heat the fry oil to 350° to 375°F over medium heat. Working in batches as needed, fry the potatoes again until golden brown and crispy, moving them around for even cooking, 3 to 4 minutes. Return to the wire rack and sprinkle with salt.

Meanwhile, add the beef broth to the skillet with the beef drippings and deglaze the pan over medium heat, scraping the bottom of the skillet. Stir in the cream, black pepper, Worcestershire sauce, mustard, and salt. Simmer until reduced and thick enough to coat the back of a spoon, 5 to 6 minutes.

Finish with the butter, stirring until glossy.

Slice the steak against the grain and plate alongside the crispy fries. Drizzle the steak with peppercorn sauce or leave on the side for dipping!

MORIBYAN'S TIP

The secret to deep-frying is patience with the oil temperature. Each time you add a new batch, the oil temperature dips a little. Always check the thermometer and wait for it to heat back up before adding more potatoes—this keeps your fries crispy instead of greasy.

PEPPERCORN SAUCE

½ cup beef broth
⅓ cup heavy cream
2 teaspoons crushed black peppercorns
2 teaspoons Worcestershire sauce
1 teaspoon yellow mustard
Pinch of salt
1 tablespoon unsalted butter

STEAK SANDWICHES
with Caramelized Onions, Arugula & Chimichurri Aioli

One bite into this decadent sandwich and you'll wonder how you ever went so long without it. Salty, umami-rich steak is topped with sweet, caramelized onions, while fresh arugula adds a peppery crunch. The real secret? A chimichurri aioli that sneaks in herbs and acid, but in a creamy, mayonnaise-based sauce that ties everything together. I truly hope this sandwich takes your breath away.

MAKES 2 SANDWICHES

CARAMELIZED ONIONS

1½ teaspoons neutral oil
½ large yellow onion, thinly sliced
Pinch of salt

CHIMICHURRI AIOLI

⅔ cup mayonnaise
¼ cup finely chopped parsley
2 tablespoons finely chopped fresh cilantro
2 tablespoons olive oil
1 tablespoon red wine vinegar
1 teaspoon minced garlic
1 teaspoon dried oregano
¾ teaspoon red pepper flakes

STEAK

12-ounce boneless rib-eye steak (1 to 1½ inches thick), at room temperature
¾ teaspoon salt
½ teaspoon freshly ground black pepper
1½ teaspoons neutral oil
1½ tablespoons butter
2 or 3 slices white American or provolone cheese

ASSEMBLY

3 cups arugula
1 tablespoon olive oil
¼ teaspoon salt
¼ teaspoon freshly ground black pepper
1 to 2 tablespoons butter, oil, or mayonnaise, for toasting the bread
2 or 3 ciabatta rolls (3 ounces each), cut in half horizontally

Make the caramelized onions: In a sauté pan, heat the oil over medium-low heat. Add the onions and salt and cook, stirring occasionally, until soft and golden brown, 20 to 30 minutes. If they start to stick, add a splash of water to deglaze the pan. Set aside.

Make the chimichurri aioli: In a bowl, stir together the mayonnaise, parsley, cilantro, olive oil, vinegar, garlic, oregano, and pepper flakes until smooth. Cover and refrigerate until ready to use.

Cook the steak: Pat the rib eye dry and season both sides with the salt and black pepper.

Heat a cast-iron skillet over high heat and coat with neutral oil. Once the oil ripples and starts to smoke, sear the fat-cap side of the steak until crispy, about 1 minute. Now sear the steak on each side for 3½ to 4 minutes for medium-rare, 4 to 5 minutes for medium to medium-well, and 5 to 6 minutes for well done. Reduce the heat to medium-low, add the butter, and baste for 1 more minute.

Remove from the heat and let the steak rest for at least 5 to 10 minutes before slicing thinly against the grain.

Assemble the sandwiches: Preheat the oven to 400°F.

In a bowl, toss the arugula with olive oil, salt, and black pepper.

Spread butter, oil, or mayonnaise on the cut sides of the ciabatta. Reheat the cast-iron skillet (or a clean nonstick, if you want) over medium heat and toast the bread, cut-side down, until golden and crisp, 1 to 2 minutes.

Spread a generous layer of chimichurri aioli on the top halves of each toasted ciabatta and set them aside. Arrange the sliced steak on the bottom halves, then add cheese slices over the steak. Place just the bottom halves on a sheet pan and broil for about 2 minutes, until the cheese melts and the bread is toasty. Once out of the oven, spoon the caramelized onions on top of the melted cheese, add the seasoned arugula, and close the sandwiches with the reserved ciabatta tops. Press gently, cut in half, and enjoy!

GRILLED KOREAN-STYLE SHORT RIBS

Growing up in Orange County, I was surrounded by incredible Korean BBQ spots, and the bone-in short ribs were always my go-to order. When I visited Seoul, I had to try them there, too, and they instantly became my favorite. Each bite was tender, juicy, and just a little sweet from the pear in the marinade. The Asian pear doesn't just add sweetness, it also tenderizes the beef, so the meat grills up juicy and melt-in-your-mouth. Marinate the ribs in the morning and by evening they're perfectly seasoned and ready to grill for dinner. I love serving them with jasmine rice and the Hawaiian-Inspired Garlic Shrimp with Mac Salad (page 153) for a full spread.

SERVES 4 TO 6

MARINATED RIBS

- ½ Asian pear, core removed
- ½ yellow onion
- ½ cup reduced-sodium soy sauce
- ⅓ cup dark brown sugar
- 3 tablespoons rice vinegar
- 1 tablespoon toasted sesame oil
- 2 tablespoons minced garlic
- 1 tablespoon minced fresh ginger or ginger paste
- 1 teaspoon freshly ground black pepper
- 4 green onions, green part only, cut into 2- to 3-inch pieces
- 3 pounds bone-in short ribs, about 12 pieces

FOR SERVING

- 2 green onions, thinly sliced, for garnish
- Toasted sesame seeds, for garnish

Marinate the ribs: In a blender or food processor, blend the Asian pear and onion until smooth.

In a large bowl, whisk together the soy sauce, brown sugar, rice vinegar, sesame oil, garlic, ginger, and black pepper. Stir in the blended pear/onion mixture and add the chopped green onions.

Arrange the short ribs in a long tray big enough for them to lie flat. Pour the marinade over the ribs, ensuring they are fully coated. Cover and refrigerate for at least 6 hours or overnight for the most tender meat.

Preheat a grill or grill pan over medium-high heat. Remove the ribs from the marinade, letting the excess drip off.

Cook the short ribs for about 3 minutes per side for medium doneness or 4 minutes per side for a more well-done finish.

Let the ribs rest for a few minutes before serving, garnished with green onions and sesame seeds.

RESTAURANT REMAKES

AUNTIE ANNE'S SOFT PRETZELS

with Honey Mustard Dip

This recipe is for anyone who spent weekends hanging out at the mall or amusement park, with the irresistible smell of Auntie Anne's or Wetzel Pretzel in the air.

My goal was to re-create that soft, buttery pretzel from my childhood but make it simpler. A lot of recipes require boiling the pretzels after shaping them, but we're skipping that step, just like what I saw in Philly. Instead, the pretzels are dipped in a baking soda/hot water bath, which is easier than fully boiling them but tastes just as delicious.

MAKES 8 PRETZELS

HONEY MUSTARD SAUCE

- ⅓ cup mayonnaise
- 1 tablespoon yellow mustard
- 1 tablespoon Dijon mustard
- 2½ tablespoons honey
- 1½ teaspoons fresh lemon juice
- ¼ teaspoon paprika

DOUGH

- 1¼ cups (310g) lukewarm milk
- 2 tablespoons sugar
- 2 teaspoons instant yeast
- 3¼ cups (455g) all-purpose flour
- 3 tablespoons unsalted butter, melted
- 1 teaspoon salt
- Neutral oil, for greasing the bowl

TO FINISH

- ¼ cup baking soda
- 4 cups boiling hot water
- ½ to 1 tablespoon pretzel salt
- 4 tablespoons (2 ounces/55g) unsalted butter, melted

Make the honey mustard sauce: In a small bowl, combine the mayonnaise, yellow mustard, Dijon mustard, honey, lemon juice, and paprika. Whisk until smooth, then taste and adjust the honey or mustard if you want it sweeter or tangier. Cover and set aside in the fridge.

Make the dough: In a large bowl, combine the lukewarm milk, sugar, and yeast. Cover and let it sit until foamy on top, about 10 minutes.

In a stand mixer fitted with the dough hook (or in a large bowl working by hand), combine the flour, melted butter, and salt and knead on medium speed until a soft dough forms, 5 to 6 minutes. (If kneading by hand, turn the dough out onto a lightly floured surface and knead until it becomes smooth and elastic, 8 to 9 minutes.)

Transfer to a large, lightly oiled bowl, cover, and let it rise in a warm place until doubled in size, about 1 hour.

Punch down the dough, transfer to a clean work surface, and divide into 8 equal pieces. Roll each piece into a rope about 3 feet long.

To shape into pretzels, form a U-shape with the rope, cross the ends over each other twice to form a twist, fold the twisted ends down, and press them under the bottom of the U to seal it tightly.

Preheat the oven to 450°F. Grease a nonstick baking sheet with a little oil (or use parchment paper if your tray isn't nonstick).

To finish: In a wide dish, mix the baking soda with the hot water. Make sure it's not too hot to touch. Dunk each pretzel and immediately transfer to the prepared baking sheet. While the pretzels are still wet, sprinkle pretzel salt on top.

Bake until puffed and golden brown, 9 to 11 minutes. As soon as they're out, brush with melted butter and serve warm.

DIN TAI FUNG CUCUMBER SALAD

Din Tai Fung is a popular Taiwanese chain most famous for its soup dumplings, or xiaolongbao. I ate there when I visited Taipei, and the dish that totally blew me away was the cucumber salad. It was so good, we ended up ordering three plates. My version is super easy to make at home. Just slice the cucumbers into coins and salt them to drain out excess water and bitterness, leaving you with a crisp texture. Let them chill in the fridge and enjoy them with almost anything or just snack on them as is. That's how good they are.

SERVES 4

- 6 Persian (mini) cucumbers (about 1 pound total), cut into rounds ½ inch thick
- Salt
- 2 teaspoons toasted sesame oil
- 2 tablespoons reduced-sodium soy sauce
- 2 teaspoons chili oil
- 1 teaspoon minced garlic
- 2 tablespoons rice vinegar
- 1 tablespoon sugar
- ½ Fresno chile, finely diced

Place the cucumbers in a large bowl and toss them with 1½ teaspoons salt. Let them sit for about 30 minutes. This helps draw out excess moisture and gives the cucumbers that perfect crisp bite. Drain out the water at the bottom of the bowl.

After draining, gently pat the cucumbers dry with paper towels to remove any leftover moisture.

In a bowl, whisk together the sesame oil, soy sauce, chili oil, garlic, vinegar, sugar, and Fresno chile until everything is well combined.

Toss the drained cucumbers in the dressing and mix until each piece is evenly coated. Taste and add a pinch of salt if needed. Let them marinate in the fridge for at least 1 hour before serving—the longer they sit, the better the flavor. Toss every 20 minutes to ensure the cucumbers marinate evenly.

Serve cold and enjoy that sweet, tangy, spicy crunch, or store in the fridge for up to 3 days.

McDONALD'S FILET-O-FISH

Now you can skip the drive-thru, because I've developed a McDonald's classic worth staying in for. This is my take on the iconic Filet-O-Fish with a few simple upgrades that make all the difference. The tender white fish fillet is fried to perfection, so it's still juicy on the inside and crispy on the outside, while the homemade tartar sauce adds a vibrant freshness and creaminess. I like to toast the buns for extra texture, but you can steam them like McDonald's does if you prefer.

MAKES 4 SANDWICHES

TARTAR SAUCE

- 1 cup mayonnaise
- ¼ cup dill relish
- 1 tablespoon fresh lemon juice
- 1 tablespoon finely chopped fresh parsley
- ¾ teaspoon sugar
- 1 teaspoon yellow mustard
- 1 teaspoon dried dill
- ½ teaspoon onion powder
- ½ teaspoon red pepper flakes
- ½ teaspoon freshly ground black pepper

FISH FILLETS

- 4 white fish fillets (3 to 4 ounces each), such as cod, pollock, or haddock
- Salt and freshly ground black pepper
- 1 cup panko bread crumbs
- ¾ cup all-purpose flour
- 2 teaspoons chili powder
- 2 large eggs

FRYING AND ASSEMBLY

- Vegetable oil, for deep-frying
- 4 slices American cheese
- Butter, for toasting
- 4 brioche buns, split

Make the tartar sauce: In a small bowl, combine the mayonnaise, dill relish, lemon juice, parsley, sugar, mustard, dill, onion powder, pepper flakes, and black pepper. Mix well until smooth and creamy. Set aside.

Prepare the fish: Pat the fish fillets dry and season both sides with salt and black pepper. Blend the panko in a food processor just until it is more fine but not a powder. (Or crush them in a ziplock bag with a rolling pin.)

Set up a dredging station in three wide shallow bowls: In one bowl, combine the flour, ¾ teaspoon salt, ½ teaspoon black pepper, and 1 teaspoon of the chili powder and mix well. In a second bowl, beat the eggs with ½ teaspoon salt, ½ teaspoon chili powder, and ¼ teaspoon black pepper. In the third bowl, stir together the panko, ½ teaspoon salt, ¼ teaspoon black pepper, and the remaining ½ teaspoon chili powder.

Using one hand for dry ingredients and the other for wet to keep things neat, dredge each fillet in the seasoned flour, shake off the excess, then dip it into the egg mixture. Finally, press it into the seasoned panko until well coated on all sides. Set all the breaded fillets on a plate.

Fry and assemble: Set a wire rack in a sheet pan and have near the stove. Pour 2 inches vegetable oil into a deep heavy-bottomed pot and heat over medium-high heat to 350°F.

Working in batches to avoid overcrowding, gently lower the breaded fillets into the oil and fry until golden brown and crispy on both sides, 3 to 4 minutes per side, depending on thickness. Transfer to the wire rack to drain. Add a slice of cheese on top of each fillet to start melting.

Immediately after the fish is done frying, melt some butter in a skillet over medium heat. Toast the brioche buns, cut-side down, until golden, 1 to 2 minutes.

Spread a spoonful of tartar sauce on the bottom bun, then layer on the cheese-topped fish fillet, and another spoonful of tartar sauce. Top with the other bun and serve warm.

WINGSTOP HOT HONEY CHICKEN TENDERS
with Ranch

I was never really into wings, so Wingstop wasn't exactly on my radar. But that totally changed when they came out with their hot honey chicken tenders. The tenders are the best combo of sweet and spicy, with the juiciest bite inside and the crispiest coating outside. I was instantly hooked. To achieve that crispy, craggy coating in my version, I mix a little of the wet batter into the flour. It creates those golden, flaky bits that cling to every inch of the chicken and give you that perfect crunch.

SERVES 4

FINISHING SPICE

- 2¼ teaspoons paprika
- 2¼ teaspoons chili powder
- ¾ teaspoon cayenne pepper
- 1½ teaspoons freshly ground black pepper
- ¾ teaspoon salt

HOT HONEY SAUCE

- 12 tablespoons unsalted butter
- 6 tablespoons hot sauce
- ½ cup honey
- ¾ teaspoon cayenne pepper

WET BATTER

- ¾ cup buttermilk
- 1 large egg
- 1 teaspoon salt
- ½ teaspoon freshly ground black pepper
- ¼ teaspoon cayenne pepper

DRY BREADING

- 1½ cups all-purpose flour
- ⅓ cup cornstarch
- 3 teaspoons paprika
- 2 teaspoons salt
- 1½ teaspoons mustard powder
- 1½ teaspoons garlic powder
- 1 teaspoon baking powder
- ¾ teaspoon onion powder
- ¾ teaspoon freshly ground black pepper
- ½ teaspoon cayenne pepper

Make the finishing spice: In a small bowl, combine the paprika, chili powder, cayenne, black pepper, and salt. Set aside.

Make the hot honey sauce: In a small saucepan, melt the butter over low heat. Whisk in the hot sauce, honey, cayenne, and 1½ teaspoons of the finishing spice. Let it bubble gently for 1 to 2 minutes until smooth and glossy. Remove from the heat and set aside for later.

Make the wet batter: In a medium bowl, combine the buttermilk, egg, salt, black pepper, and cayenne. Whisk until completely smooth and combined. Set aside.

Make the dry breading: In a large shallow bowl or dish, combine the flour, cornstarch, paprika, salt, mustard powder, garlic powder, baking powder, onion powder, black pepper, and cayenne. Whisk well to evenly combine.

Add 3 tablespoons of the prepared wet batter into the dry breading. Use your fingers to massage the wet into the dry mix to form flakes. These clumps will create the crispy, craggy bits on the chicken coating.

RECIPE & INGREDIENTS CONTINUE

Cook the chicken tenders: Pat the chicken tenders dry using paper towels. Dredge each piece in the dry breading, pressing gently to adhere. Dip into the wet batter, fully coating the tender. Return to the dry breading, packing the flour mixture and clumps onto the chicken for maximum texture. Place the coated tenders on a tray and let them rest for at least 30 minutes while you heat the oil.

Fit a sheet pan with a wire rack or line with paper towels and have near the stove. Pour 2 inches of vegetable oil into a deep heavy-bottomed pot and heat to 350°F.

Working in batches, carefully lower the tenders into the hot oil and fry until deeply golden and cooked through (internal temp should be 165°F), 5 to 6 minutes. Transfer to the wire rack or paper towels to drain.

Place the fried tenders in a large bowl. Pour the hot honey sauce over them and toss to coat evenly. Sprinkle all over with the finishing spice.

Serve immediately with chilled ranch on the side.

MORIBYAN'S TIP

To make sure the breading actually sticks, pat the chicken dry really well, and once you coat the tenders, let them rest for at least 15 minutes before frying so the crust sets.

CHICKEN TENDERS

- 12 chicken breast tenders (about 1½ pounds)
- Vegetable oil, for frying
- Wingstop Ranch (recipe follows), chilled, for serving

WINGSTOP RANCH

In a medium bowl, combine the buttermilk, mayo, Worcestershire sauce, mustard, dried parsley, dill, chives, garlic powder, onion powder, black pepper, and pepper flakes. Whisk everything together until smooth and creamy.

Taste and adjust the seasoning if you like, adding a little more dill for extra freshness or a pinch more red pepper flakes for a kick. Once it's all well mixed, refrigerate for at least 30 minutes to let the flavors meld together. Store it in an airtight container in the fridge for up to 1 week.

MAKES 2 CUPS

- 1 cup buttermilk
- 1 cup mayonnaise
- 1½ teaspoons Worcestershire sauce
- 1 teaspoon yellow mustard
- 1 teaspoon dried parsley
- ½ teaspoon finely chopped fresh dill
- ½ teaspoon finely chopped fresh chives
- ½ teaspoon garlic powder
- ½ teaspoon onion powder
- ½ teaspoon freshly ground black pepper
- Pinch of red pepper flakes

MENDOCINO FARMS NOT-SO-FRIED CHICKEN SANDWICHES

Mendocino Farms started in Los Angeles about an hour from where I grew up in Orange County and I used to drive all the way there just for this sandwich. When they finally opened one closer to home, it was game over. I was so obsessed that one summer I even got a job there just so I could eat the food every single day. Now this sandwich isn't your average sandwich. The chicken is thinly shaved and layered with the most insane crispy bits that I worked so hard to try to replicate. It's topped with tangy pickled onions, creamy coleslaw with pickles and mustard, and an herb aioli so good you'll want to eat it with a spoon—all piled onto toasted ciabatta and served with a side of BBQ sauce. There is truly no sandwich more perfect or special than this.

MAKES 4 SANDWICHES

PICKLED RED ONIONS

- ½ red onion, thinly sliced
- ½ cup hot water
- ½ cup distilled white vinegar
- 2 tablespoons sugar
- ½ teaspoon salt

TANGY COLESLAW

- ⅓ cup mayonnaise
- 2 tablespoons pickle relish
- 1 tablespoon yellow mustard
- 1 tablespoon apple cider vinegar
- 1 tablespoon sugar
- ¼ teaspoon salt, or to taste
- ¼ teaspoon black pepper
- 3 cups coleslaw mix

HERB AIOLI

- ½ cup mayonnaise
- ¼ cup chopped fresh parsley
- 1 tablespoon chopped fresh dill
- 1 tablespoon fresh lemon juice
- 1 garlic clove, minced or finely grated

Make the pickled red onions: Place the red onions in a small jar or bowl. In a cup, whisk together the hot water, vinegar, sugar, and salt until the sugar and salt dissolve. Pour the liquid over the sliced onions, making sure they're fully submerged. Let them sit for at least 30 minutes while you prep everything else. (These can be made up to 1 week in advance and stored in the fridge.)

Make the tangy coleslaw: In a large bowl, whisk together the mayo, pickle relish, mustard, vinegar, sugar, salt, and black pepper until smooth. Add the slaw mix and toss until every piece is coated. Set in the fridge to chill and let the flavors meld together.

Make the herb aioli: In a small bowl, combine the mayo, parsley, dill, lemon juice, and garlic. Mix until smooth and creamy. Store in the fridge until ready to use.

RECIPE & INGREDIENTS CONTINUE

Cook the chicken: In a bowl, toss the chicken breasts with the oil, salt, garlic powder, onion powder, smoked paprika, and black pepper.

Heat a skillet over medium-high heat. Add the chicken and cook until golden brown on both sides, about 6 minutes per side. Reduce the heat to medium-low, cover, and cook until fully cooked in the center of the thickest part of the chicken, about 2 to 3 minutes.

Remove from the heat, rest for 10 minutes, and then very thinly slice to look like shaved chicken.

Assemble the sandwiches: Spread herb aioli on both the top and bottom halves of the toasted ciabatta. Sprinkle a few krispies on the bottom. Add the chicken and add a few more krispies on top. Add a layer of pickled red onions, then spoon on a big scoop of coleslaw and gently press it down. Lay a few slices of tomato on top and season them with a little salt and pepper. Close the sandwich with the top piece of bread, press lightly, and slice in half to enjoy!

PAN-GRILLED CHICKEN

- 1 pound boneless, skinless chicken breasts
- 1 tablespoon neutral oil
- ¾ teaspoon salt
- ½ teaspoon garlic powder
- ½ teaspoon onion powder
- ½ teaspoon smoked paprika
- ¼ teaspoon freshly ground black pepper

ASSEMBLY

- 4 sandwich-size loaves ciabatta bread, split in half and toasted
- Mendo Krispies (recipe follows)
- 1 to 2 tomatoes, thinly sliced
- Salt and freshly ground black pepper

MENDO KRISPIES

In a bowl, mix the crumbled polenta, flour, Parmesan, cornstarch, buttermilk, oregano, black pepper, parsley, and salt until fully combined.

Line a plate with paper towels and have near the stove. Pour 2 inches vegetable oil into a deep heavy-bottomed pot and heat over medium-high heat to 350°F.

Working in batches to avoid overcrowding, carefully sprinkle in the mixture and fry until golden and crisp, 6 to 8 minutes. Remove with a slotted spoon and drain on the paper towels, seasoning to taste with salt. If any of your pieces are larger than you'd like, you can crumble them into smaller pieces. Store them in an airtight container at room temperature for up to 5 days.

MAKES ABOUT 2¼ CUPS

- 8 ounces cooked polenta, crumbled fine
- ¼ cup all-purpose flour
- ¼ cup freshly grated Parmesan cheese
- 2 tablespoons cornstarch
- 1 tablespoon buttermilk
- ½ teaspoon dried oregano
- ¼ teaspoon freshly ground black pepper
- ½ teaspoon chopped fresh parsley
- ¼ teaspoon salt, plus more to finish
- Vegetable oil, for deep-frying

NANDO'S PERI PERI CHICKEN & RICE

Nando's started in South Africa and became a huge part of the UK food scene. I was always so into British culture growing up that I even dreamed of moving to London, so when I finally got to visit, trying Nando's was at the top of my list.

One bite of their peri peri chicken with that flavorful rice, and I was hooked. The chicken is perfectly charred, packed with spices, and has just the right kick—not too spicy, but loaded with flavor. The secret? Peri peri sauce, a hot sauce made from bird's eye chiles. That chile can be tough to find, so instead of making the sauce from scratch, I'd just grab a bottle from the store. Plus, you get to pick your perfect spice level!

Honestly, who needs a flight across the pond when you can make this version at home?

SERVES 4

PERI PERI CHICKEN

- 1 tablespoon olive oil
- 2 teaspoons chili powder
- 1 teaspoon smoked paprika
- 1 teaspoon garlic powder
- ¾ teaspoon salt
- ½ teaspoon freshly ground black pepper
- ½ teaspoon ground cumin
- 1½ pounds boneless, skinless chicken thighs
- ¼ cup mild or medium peri peri sauce

SPICY RICE

- 1 tablespoon olive oil
- 1 tablespoon unsalted butter
- 1 red bell pepper, chopped
- ½ yellow onion, chopped
- 2 teaspoons minced garlic
- 1 tablespoon tomato paste
- 1½ cups jasmine rice, rinsed well and drained
- 2¼ cups chicken broth
- 2 teaspoons chili powder
- 1 teaspoon paprika
- 1 teaspoon ground turmeric
- 1 teaspoon salt
- ½ teaspoon dried oregano
- ½ to ¾ teaspoon red pepper flakes, to taste
- 1 cup green peas
- 1 tablespoon chopped fresh cilantro

Make the peri peri chicken: In a large bowl, stir to mix the olive oil, chili powder, smoked paprika, garlic powder, salt, black pepper, and cumin. Add the chicken thighs and turn to coat evenly.

Heat a large nonstick sauté pan over medium-high heat. Add the chicken and cook until golden and firm and the internal temperature reaches 165°F, 4 to 5 minutes per side.

Brush the top of the chicken with peri peri sauce and flip over so the sauce caramelizes slightly, about 1 minute. Brush the other side, flip over again, and cook for another minute. Remove from the heat, cover, and set aside on a plate to keep warm.

Make the spicy rice: In a clean pan, heat the olive oil and butter over medium heat. Add the bell pepper and onion and cook until slightly softened, 4 to 5 minutes.

Stir in the garlic and sauté for 30 seconds until fragrant. Add the tomato paste and sauté another 1 to 2 minutes to remove the acidity.

Add the rinsed jasmine rice and toast for 1 minute. Add the chicken broth, chili powder, paprika, turmeric, salt, oregano, and pepper flakes. Stir well and bring to a simmer. Reduce the heat to low, cover, and cook until all the liquid is absorbed, about 15 minutes.

Turn off the heat, add the green peas on top, and quickly re-cover the pan for 10 minutes to steam the rice and peas. Fluff the rice with a fork, add the chopped cilantro, and give it a quick mix.

Cut the chicken thighs into strips. To serve, place some rice on a serving plate and top with the chicken.

HALAL CART CHICKEN & YELLOW RICE

The first time I visited New York City I couldn't wait to try one of the iconic halal carts. You'll find chains like Halal Guys in other cities, but nothing hits quite like the independently run ones in NYC. It's crazy how you get a giant platter of spiced chicken, fluffy rice, crisp salad, and that addicting white sauce all for under ten bucks. I even waited over an hour once, which is when I decided to develop my own version at home. Now we barely even buy it in the city anymore because this copycat satisfies every craving. The real secret? That white sauce. It's like a thinner, mayo-y version of toum, Lebanese garlic paste, and once you taste it, you'll want to drizzle it on everything, from wraps to salads.

SERVES 4

WHITE SAUCE

- ½ cup mayonnaise
- ¼ cup sour cream or yogurt
- 1 tablespoon fresh lemon juice, or more to taste
- 1 teaspoon minced garlic
- ½ teaspoon sugar
- ½ teaspoon freshly ground black pepper, or more to taste

CHICKEN

- 2 tablespoons olive oil, plus more for pan
- 1½ teaspoons ground allspice
- 1 teaspoon ground coriander
- 1 teaspoon garlic powder
- 1 teaspoon paprika
- 1 teaspoon ground cumin
- 1 teaspoon salt, or to taste
- 1 teaspoon sumac
- ¼ teaspoon freshly ground black pepper
- ¼ teaspoon ground turmeric
- 1½ pounds boneless, skinless chicken thighs

YELLOW RICE

- 2 tablespoons unsalted butter
- 2 cups basmati rice, rinsed well
- 3 cups chicken broth
- ½ teaspoon ground turmeric
- ½ teaspoon dried oregano
- ½ teaspoon ground cumin
- 1½ teaspoons salt
- 1 bay leaf

FOR SERVING

- Shredded lettuce
- Diced tomatoes
- Sriracha or hot sauce

Make the white sauce: In a small bowl, whisk together the mayonnaise, sour cream, lemon juice, garlic, sugar, black pepper, and 2 tablespoons water until smooth. Taste and adjust the seasoning, adding more pepper or lemon juice if needed.

Cook the chicken: In a bowl, combine the olive oil, allspice, coriander, garlic powder, paprika, cumin, salt, sumac, black pepper, and turmeric. Coat the chicken thighs evenly with the spice mixture. (Optional: Cover with plastic wrap and marinate in the fridge for at least 30 minutes, or up to overnight in the fridge for more flavor.)

Heat a skillet over medium-high heat, add a drizzle of oil, and cook the chicken thighs until cooked through and golden brown, 6 to 7 minutes per side. The internal temperature should reach 165°F. Remove from the pan and let it rest for a few minutes before cutting up.

Make the yellow rice: In a medium saucepan, melt the butter over medium heat. Add the rice, stir to coat, and toast for 1 to 2 minutes.

Add the chicken broth, turmeric, oregano, cumin, salt, and bay leaf. Stir to combine and bring the mixture to a boil. Reduce the heat to low, cover, and simmer until the rice is tender and all the liquid is absorbed, 15 to 18 minutes. Take off the heat but leave covered for 10 minutes to steam the rice. Uncover, remove the bay leaf, and fluff the rice with a fork.

To serve: Plate the yellow rice with lettuce and tomatoes, top with the cut-up chicken, and drizzle with the white sauce and sriracha. Serve warm and enjoy!

COSTCO CHICKEN BAKE

The Costco Chicken Bake is a cult favorite from their food court, consisting of cheese, bacon, chicken, and creamy Caesar dressing wrapped in a burrito-shaped dough shell that is topped with cheese and baked. Growing up, I used to eye the food court chicken bakes longingly but I could never try one because of the bacon. In my take, I use all-beef bacon here and give you the option of using store-bought or homemade pizza dough!

MAKES FOUR 8-INCH BAKES

CAESAR DRESSING

- ½ cup mayonnaise
- 2 tablespoons buttermilk
- 1½ teaspoons fresh lemon juice
- 1 teaspoon Worcestershire sauce
- 1 teaspoon minced garlic
- 1 teaspoon yellow mustard
- 1 teaspoon dried parsley
- ½ teaspoon freshly ground black pepper
- ¼ cup freshly grated Parmesan cheese

CHICKEN

- 2 tablespoons olive or avocado oil
- 1 teaspoon chili powder
- 1 teaspoon salt
- ½ teaspoon garlic powder
- ½ teaspoon onion powder
- ½ teaspoon freshly ground black pepper
- 1 pound boneless, skinless chicken breasts

ASSEMBLY

- 1 pound pizza dough, homemade (see page 205) or store-bought
- All-purpose flour, for rolling
- 6 ounces beef bacon, cooked and chopped
- 2 cups shredded mozzarella cheese
- 2 tablespoons finely chopped fresh parsley
- Egg wash: 1 large egg beaten with 2 tablespoons heavy cream
- ¼ cup grated Parmesan cheese
- Italian seasoning
- Garlic powder

Make the Caesar dressing: In a small bowl, mix together the mayo, buttermilk, lemon juice, Worcestershire sauce, garlic, mustard, parsley, black pepper, and Parmesan until smooth. Set aside.

Cook the chicken: In a small bowl, mix 1 tablespoon of the olive oil with the chili powder, salt, garlic powder, onion powder, and black pepper. Pour the marinade over the chicken breasts so every piece is coated.

In a skillet, heat the remaining 1 tablespoon oil over medium-high heat. Add the chicken and cook until golden brown on both sides, 4 to 5 minutes per side. Lower the heat and cook until the internal temperature reaches 165°F, 2 to 3 minutes. Once cooked, set aside to rest for about 5 minutes before cutting into small chunks.

Assemble and bake: Preheat the oven to 425°F.

Divide the dough into 4 equal 4-ounce portions. If the dough is sticky, dust your surface, rolling pin, and dough with all-purpose flour as needed. Roll out each piece into a large round 8 to 9 inches across.

Spread 2 to 3 tablespoons of Caesar dressing in the center of each dough round. Add about ⅔ cup chopped chicken and 2 to 3 tablespoons cooked bacon on top, followed by ⅓ cup of shredded mozzarella and a light sprinkle of chopped parsley. You can also drizzle a little more Caesar dressing on top if you'd like it extra saucy. To wrap, fold the left and right sides of the dough in toward the center so they just overlap the filling. Next, fold the edge closest to you up and over the filling, then roll it away from you, tucking in the filling as you go, until you have a snug, sealed log—just like wrapping a burrito. Pinch any open seams to help keep everything contained while baking. Each bake should be 8 to 9 inches long.

Place the bakes seam-side down on a parchment-lined baking sheet. Brush each rolled dough with the egg wash. Top with 2 to 3 tablespoons of shredded mozzarella and a light dusting of Parmesan. Sprinkle Italian seasoning and a touch of garlic powder over the top.

Bake until golden, cheesy, and crispy on top, 17 to 20 minutes. Remove from the oven and let cool slightly before serving.

BONCHON KOREAN-STYLE FRIED CHICKEN
with Two Sauces

I grew up in a city with a big Korean American community, so I got introduced to the cuisine early, and ever since then, it's been one of my favorites. When I finally visited South Korea, I was so excited to eat all my favorite foods in the place where they were created. One of the most iconic dishes is Korean fried chicken. It's double-fried for that signature crunch, and even at home, you'll see how much crispier it gets after the second fry. Traditional versions use potato and rice starch, but I wanted to keep it simple with just all-purpose flour and cornstarch, and it still stays super crispy. I even let it sit for two hours and no crisp was lost! And we couldn't forget the two classic sauces with honey garlic bringing something buttery and sweet and gochujang adding the perfect spicy kick.

SERVES 4 TO 6

GOCHUJANG GLAZE

- ¼ cup gochujang
- ¼ cup light brown sugar
- 2 tablespoons honey
- 2 tablespoons reduced-sodium soy sauce
- 1 tablespoon unsalted butter
- 1 tablespoon rice vinegar
- 1½ teaspoons finely minced garlic
- ½ teaspoon red pepper flakes or gochugaru
- 1 teaspoon toasted sesame oil

HONEY SOY GLAZE

- 4 tablespoons unsalted butter
- 1 tablespoon minced garlic
- 3 to 4 tablespoons honey, to taste
- 3 tablespoons reduced-sodium soy sauce
- 2 tablespoons rice vinegar
- ½ teaspoon freshly ground black pepper
- Cornstarch slurry: 1 teaspoon cornstarch whisked with 2 tablespoons water

MARINATED CHICKEN

- 2 pounds boneless, skinless chicken thighs, cut into 1½-inch chunks
- 1 tablespoon reduced-sodium soy sauce
- 1 teaspoon rice vinegar
- 1 teaspoon minced garlic
- 1 teaspoon salt
- ½ teaspoon freshly ground black pepper

Make the gochujang glaze: In a small saucepan, combine the gochujang, brown sugar, honey, soy sauce, butter, vinegar, garlic, pepper flakes, sesame oil, and ¼ cup water. Whisk together until well combined and simmer until the glaze thickens and becomes glossy, 5 to 6 minutes. Remove from the heat and set aside.

Make the honey soy glaze: In another small saucepan, melt the butter over medium heat. Add the garlic and cook for 1 to 2 minutes, until fragrant. Stir in 3 tablespoons of the honey, the soy sauce, vinegar, and black pepper. Bring to a simmer and cook for 3 to 4 minutes. Add the cornstarch slurry and cook until the glaze thickens, an additional 2 minutes. Taste and adjust the sweetness to your liking with more honey. Remove from the heat and set aside.

Marinate the chicken: In a medium bowl, combine the chicken thighs with the soy sauce, vinegar, garlic, salt, and black pepper. Toss until evenly coated and let it marinate for at least 10 to 15 minutes while you prepare the dredge.

RECIPE & INGREDIENTS CONTINUE

Make the wet batter: In a medium bowl, whisk together the water, flour, cornstarch, paprika, baking powder, salt, and pepper.

Make the dry breading: In a large sealed container or ziplock bag, combine the cornstarch, flour, baking powder, paprika, salt, and pepper.

Once the chicken has marinated, dip all the chicken pieces at once into the wet batter, ensuring they're fully coated.

Use your hands or kitchen tongs to lift the chicken out of the wet batter, allowing any excess to drip back into the batter, then transfer into the dry breading container or ziplock bag. Seal the bag tightly and shake vigorously until all the chicken pieces are fully coated.

To finish: Set a wire rack in a sheet pan and have near the stove. Pour 3 inches vegetable oil into a deep heavy-bottomed pot and heat over medium heat to 350°F.

Working in batches to avoid overcrowding, fry the chicken until lightly golden, 5 to 6 minutes. Set aside on the wire rack.

Raise the oil temperature to 375°F and, again working in batches, fry a second time until super crispy and golden brown, 2 to 3 more minutes.

Divide the crispy chicken into two bowls. Pour the gochujang glaze over one and the honey soy glaze over the other. Garnish the honey soy with some toasted sesame seeds and the gochujang with green onions. Toss until every piece is beautifully coated, then serve!

WET BATTER

- 1 cup ice cold water
- ½ cup all-purpose flour
- ½ cup cornstarch
- ¾ teaspoon paprika
- ½ teaspoon baking powder
- ½ teaspoon salt
- ½ teaspoon freshly ground black pepper

DRY BREADING

- 1 cup cornstarch
- ¼ cup all-purpose flour
- 1 teaspoon baking powder
- ¾ teaspoon paprika
- ½ teaspoon salt
- ½ teaspoon freshly ground black pepper

TO FINISH

- Vegetable oil, for deep-frying
- Toasted sesame seeds, for garnish
- Green onions, thinly sliced, for garnish

CAVA BRAISED LAMB

For those who don't know, Cava is a Mediterranean fast-casual spot known for its bowls and pita wraps—and their braised lamb, which everyone loves. I tested this recipe multiple times over the course of a year, and I knew it wasn't ready until I took a bite and was left speechless. Finding a whole lamb shoulder can be difficult, but I found the best hack: You can make this using lamb shoulder chops. Going back to my roots, I wanted to incorporate the sweet elements common in Moroccan lamb tagines, so you'll notice Medjool dates in my version. The final product yields tender, melt-in-your-mouth lamb with the perfect balance of savory and sweet. This dish takes time, but it's mostly unattended.

SERVES 4 TO 6

SEASONING BLEND

- 1 tablespoon paprika
- 2 teaspoons ground coriander
- 2 teaspoons salt
- 1 teaspoon onion powder
- 1 teaspoon dried mint
- 1 teaspoon freshly ground black pepper
- 1 teaspoon sumac
- ¼ teaspoon ground cardamom
- ¼ teaspoon cayenne pepper

LAMB

- 3½ to 4 pounds lamb shoulder chops
- 3 tablespoons olive oil
- 4 cups beef broth
- ½ large red onion, diced small
- 1 tablespoon minced garlic
- ¼ cup tomato paste
- 1 cinnamon stick
- 4 to 5 sprigs thyme
- 1 sprig rosemary
- 7 Medjool dates, pitted and split in half

Preheat the oven to 325°F.

Make the seasoning blend: In a small bowl, mix together all the spices. Sprinkle generously on all sides of the lamb shoulder chops. Any leftover seasoning can be added to the broth later.

Cook the lamb: In a large Dutch oven or heavy-bottomed pot, heat the olive oil over medium-high heat. Working in batches, sear the lamb chops until deeply browned, 3 to 4 minutes per side. Set aside.

Reduce the heat to medium-low and pour in ½ cup of the beef broth to deglaze the pot, scraping up all the browned bits from the bottom.

Add the onion, garlic, and tomato paste. Cook, stirring frequently with a wooden spoon or silicone spatula, until the tomato paste caramelizes and darkens, 5 to 7 minutes.

RECIPE CONTINUES

Add the cinnamon stick, thyme, rosemary, dates, and any leftover seasoning blend to the pot. Pour in the remaining 3½ cups beef broth. Mix everything together. Return the seared lamb chops to the pot. Raise the heat to medium and bring the liquid to a boil. Once boiling, remove the pot from the heat, cover, and transfer to the oven. Braise for 2 hours.

Uncover and continue cooking until the meat falls off the bone and shreds easily, 30 minutes to 1 hour (this also helps reduce the sauce and brown the meat).

Remove from the oven and carefully use tongs to transfer the lamb to a large bowl. Discard the bones and then shred the meat with two forks or tongs.

Discard the cinnamon stick and any herb stems from the broth in the pot. Strain the braising liquid through a fine-mesh sieve into a saucepan. If you'd like, you can separate out the softened onions and dates, which will have turned into a jam-like mixture—save this to dollop on top of the shredded lamb if you'd like more sweetness.

If desired, you can skim off any oil that rises to the surface of the strained sauce. At this point, you can serve the sauce as is or simmer it gently to reduce and intensify the flavor before serving.

Serve the shredded lamb with the sauce and onion/date mixture on the side, encouraging your guests to put as much as they'd like on top, then add to rice bowls or pita wraps!

TACO BELL CHEESY GORDITA CRUNCH

I couldn't have a restaurant remake chapter and NOT feature Taco Bell! A Gordita Crunch combines a crunchy hard taco shell and a soft flour tortilla for the best of both worlds, all glued together with ooey-gooey cheese. Mine is surprisingly quick and easy to make at home—like, thirty minutes easy—and the ground beef is super seasoned, saucy, and juicy. Then comes the spicy ranch, sealing the deal with the perfect creamy little spicy kick.

MAKES 6 TACOS TO SERVE 3

GROUND BEEF FILLING

- 1 tablespoon olive oil
- 1 pound ground beef (90/10)
- 2 teaspoons minced garlic
- 2 teaspoons chili powder
- 1 teaspoon ground coriander
- 1 teaspoon smoked paprika
- 1 teaspoon ground cumin
- 1 teaspoon dried oregano
- ¾ teaspoon salt, or to taste
- ½ teaspoon freshly ground black pepper
- ¼ teaspoon onion powder
- ¼ cup tomato sauce
- ¼ cup beef broth

SPICY RANCH

- ¼ cup ranch dressing
- ¼ cup sour cream
- 2 tablespoons mayonnaise
- 1 to 2 tablespoons sauce from canned chipotles in adobo, to taste
- 1 tablespoon finely chopped fresh cilantro

ASSEMBLY

- 6 (5-inch) flour tortillas
- 4 ounces cheddar cheese, shredded, plus more for topping
- 4 ounces Monterey Jack cheese, shredded
- 6 hard taco shells
- 2 cups shredded iceberg lettuce

Make the ground beef filling: Heat a skillet over medium heat and add the olive oil. Once hot, add the ground beef and break it up with a spatula. While the beef is cooking, add the minced garlic, chili powder, coriander, smoked paprika, cumin, oregano, salt, black pepper, and onion powder. Stir the spices into the beef and cook until it's browned and no longer pink, 7 to 8 minutes.

Pour in the tomato sauce and beef broth, stir, and let it simmer for 3 more minutes until the beef is saucy. Remove from the heat and set aside.

Make the spicy ranch: In a small bowl, whisk together the ranch dressing, sour cream, mayo, 1 tablespoon of the chipotle adobo sauce, and the cilantro until smooth and creamy. Taste and adjust the spice level by adding a little more chipotle if you want it spicier.

Assemble: Preheat the oven to 350°F.

Arrange the soft tortillas, without overlapping them, flat on a baking sheet.

In a medium bowl, mix both cheeses together. Sprinkle a generous handful of cheese over each flour tortilla, covering the surface evenly. Arrange the hard taco shells on another baking sheet. Warm everything in the oven just until the cheese is melted and the hard shells are heated through, 6 to 7 minutes.

Once out of the oven, immediately wrap each cheesy tortilla around a hard taco shell, gently pressing so the cheese sticks.

Fill each cheesy gordita crunch with seasoned ground beef, a drizzle of spicy ranch, shredded iceberg lettuce, and a little extra cheese if you want. Enjoy warm!

ANIMAL-STYLE IN-N-OUT BURGERS

I think it's safe to say that everyone from California grew up eating at In-N-Out. My mom would always save the extra packets of spread to take home and keep in the fridge, and she'd make her In-N-Out–style burgers from scratch at home using that sauce. So when I moved to the East Coast, where In-N-Out is nowhere to be found, that's when I knew I had to figure out how to make those iconic burgers myself just like my mom did.

MAKES 5 BURGERS

SPREAD

- ½ cup mayonnaise
- 3 tablespoons pickle relish
- ¼ cup ketchup
- 1 teaspoon yellow mustard
- 1 teaspoon sugar

CARAMELIZED ONIONS

- 1 tablespoon vegetable oil
- 1 large onion, finely diced
- ¼ teaspoon salt

PATTIES

- 1 pound ground beef (80/20)
- Salt and freshly ground black pepper
- 1 to 2 tablespoons neutral oil or unsalted butter
- 2 tablespoons yellow mustard
- 5 slices American cheese

ASSEMBLY

- 5 hamburger buns
- 2 tablespoons unsalted butter, at room temperature
- Dill pickle chips
- Tomato slices
- Shredded iceberg lettuce
- Chopped pepperoncini peppers (optional)

Make the spread: In a small bowl, mix together the mayonnaise, pickle relish, ketchup, mustard, and sugar until smooth. Cover and set aside.

Make the caramelized onions: In a sauté pan or skillet, heat the vegetable oil over medium-low heat. Add the onion and salt and cook, stirring occasionally, until the onions soften and turn a deep golden color, 15 to 20 minutes. If at any point the onions start to stick to the pan or brown aggressively rather than soften, add water, 1 tablespoon at a time, stirring each time, until the onions become perfectly caramelized and sweet. Set aside.

Make the patties: Divide the beef into 5 equal portions of about 3 ounces each. Gently shape the ground beef into balls and place them on a flat surface. Press them gently with your fingers to flatten them into thin, wide patties about ¼ inch thick. Keep in mind they will shrink as they cook. Be careful not to press or mash them too much, as that can make the burgers dense. Season the top side of each patty with salt and pepper.

Heat a skillet or griddle over medium-high heat and add a bit of neutral oil or butter. Once the pan is hot, place the patties seasoned-side down and season the top now with salt and pepper. While the first side cooks, spread a thin layer of yellow mustard on the raw side of each patty. Let them cook for 2 to 3 minutes without pressing—this keeps all those natural juices locked in. Flip the patties so the mustard side hits the pan and cook for another 2 to 3 minutes. At the last minute, add a slice of American cheese on top of each patty so it gets perfectly melty.

Assemble the burgers: While the patties are cooking, spread the buns with butter and toast them in a skillet or griddle until they're golden and crispy, 1 to 2 minutes.

Layer a generous amount of the spread on the bottom bun, then layer the toppings in this order: pickle chips, tomato slices, shredded lettuce, followed by the cheese-covered patty. Top the patty with the caramelized onions and, if you're adding them, sprinkle on the chopped pepperoncini peppers. Finally, place the top half of the bun on to complete the burger.

BENIHANA HIBACHI STEAK BOWLS

with Yum Yum Sauce

Benihana was always the spot my friends and I went to celebrate, with the chefs putting on a show of flames, fast knife work, and food flying through the air. What I loved though was the flavor—tender steak seared in garlicky butter, perfectly cooked fried rice so tasty it can be eaten by the spoonful on its own, and stir-fried veggies that looked simple but were so good. At home, this version captures all of that. Swap in chicken or shrimp for the steak, and it's just as delicious.

SERVES 4

YUM YUM SAUCE

- ½ cup mayonnaise
- ¼ cup Thai sweet chili sauce
- 1 tablespoon sriracha

FRIED RICE

- 1 tablespoon neutral oil
- ½ yellow onion, diced
- 1 tablespoon minced garlic
- ⅔ cup frozen chopped carrots
- 4 cups cooked jasmine rice, chilled
- 1 tablespoon neutral oil
- 2 large eggs, whisked
- 3 tablespoons unsalted butter
- 3 tablespoons soy sauce
- 2 teaspoons toasted sesame oil
- ¼ to ½ teaspoon salt, to taste
- ¼ teaspoon black pepper
- ¼ teaspoon granulated sugar

VEGGIES

- 1 tablespoon neutral oil
- 1 yellow onion, sliced
- 1 yellow zucchini, sliced
- 1 green zucchini, sliced
- 1 cup sliced Cremini mushrooms
- ¼ teaspoon salt
- ¼ teaspoon black pepper

STEAK

- 1½ pounds steak (NY strip, rib eye, or sirloin), cut into 1-inch cubes
- ¾ teaspoon salt
- ½ teaspoon black pepper
- 2 tablespoons unsalted butter, melted
- 2 tablespoons soy sauce
- 1 tablespoon brown sugar
- 1 tablespoon Worcestershire sauce
- 1 teaspoon minced garlic
- 2 tablespoons neutral oil

Make the yum yum sauce: In a small bowl, whisk together the mayonnaise, sweet chili sauce, and sriracha until smooth. Cover and refrigerate until you're ready to serve.

Make the fried rice: In a large skillet or wok, heat the oil over medium heat. Add the onion and sauté until soft and lightly golden, about 5 minutes. Stir in the garlic and carrots and cook for about 1 minute.

Add the rice and stir everything together. Make an opening in the center by pushing the rice out of the way, add the neutral oil, crack in the eggs, and scramble them in place until cooked. Mix the eggs into the rice, then season with the butter, soy sauce, sesame oil, salt, pepper, and granulated sugar. Mix together well and let it sit for a minute at a time to get those crispy golden bits before tossing again. Cook until evenly mixed and heated through, about 2 to 3 minutes.

Cook the veggies: Heat a large skillet over medium-high heat and drizzle in the oil. Add the onion and sauté until softened, 4 to 5 minutes. Add both zucchinis and the mushrooms, season with the salt and pepper, and stir-fry until the vegetables are tender and lightly charred, 5 to 7 minutes.

Cook the steak: In a medium bowl, toss the steak cubes with the salt and black pepper.

In a separate small bowl, combine the melted butter, soy sauce, brown sugar, Worcestershire sauce, and garlic.

Heat a large skillet or griddle over high heat and add the oil. Once hot, toss in the steak cubes and sear without moving for 2 minutes to get a golden crust. Flip and sear the other sides for another 2 minutes. Once evenly browned, pour in the sauce and cook, tossing occasionally, until the sauce is thickened and the steak is glazed and caramelized, 1 to 2 minutes.

Plate up your steak, rice, and veggies with a generous spoonful of yum yum sauce and more on the side to dig in!

ALL ABOUT THE BREAD

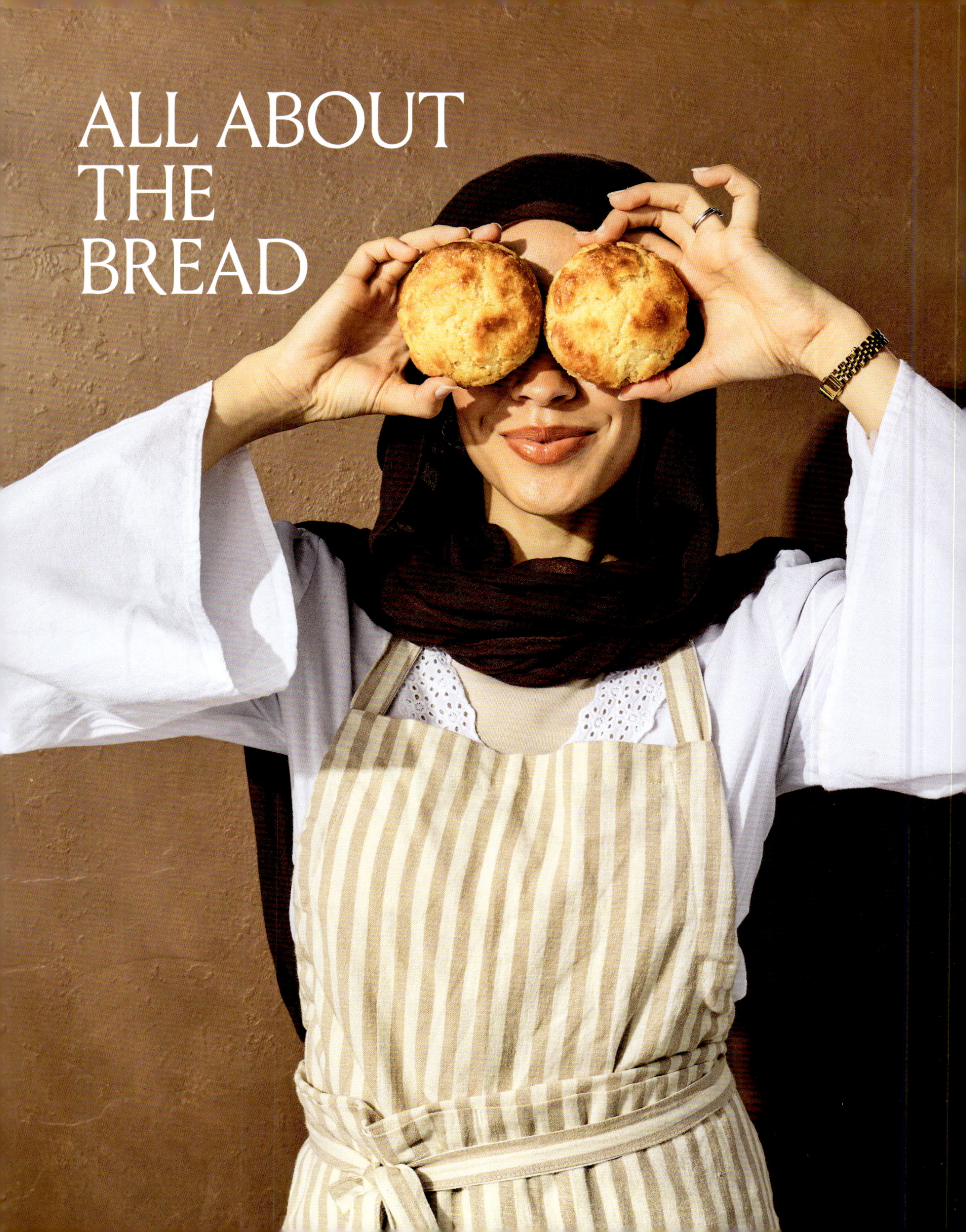

PIDESE
(Fluffy Turkish-Inspired Bread with Sesame Seeds)

This Turkish bread is soft, pillowy, and flavorful, almost like focaccia but with a more tender crust and a delicate chew. It's brushed with an egg wash for a shiny finish, scored with a crosshatch pattern, and sprinkled generously with black and white sesame seeds for a nutty crunch. The best part is that it's surprisingly easy to make, making it perfect even for new bread bakers. The shaping is fun and even a bit therapeutic, and the result looks as impressive as it tastes.

MAKES TWO 10-INCH ROUNDS

DOUGH

- ¾ cup (180g) lukewarm water
- ½ cup (120g) lukewarm whole milk
- 1 tablespoon sugar
- 2 teaspoons instant yeast
- 1 teaspoon salt
- 3 cups (420g) all-purpose flour, plus more if needed
- 1 tablespoon olive oil or ghee, for the bowl

TO FINISH

- 1 large egg
- 1 tablespoon plain yogurt
- 1 tablespoon all-purpose flour
- 2 tablespoons white and black sesame seeds

Make the dough: In the bowl of a stand mixer, combine the lukewarm water, milk, and sugar. Whisk together until the sugar is dissolved. Sprinkle the yeast on top and let it sit until frothy, about 10 minutes.

Add the salt and flour, snap on the dough hook, and knead until a soft and smooth dough forms, about 1 minute. (If you find the dough is too sticky to handle, you can add up to 3 tablespoons more flour.)

Transfer the dough to an oiled bowl and cover tightly with plastic wrap. Proof in a warm place until doubled in size, about 1 hour.

Using a bench scraper, divide the dough into 2 equal pieces. Place each dough piece on parchment paper, then roll each piece into a round about ½ inch thick. Use flour as needed on your rolling pin if it's sticking.

Cover the dough with a damp cloth and let it proof until puffy and fluffy, about 1 hour.

Adjust one rack in the lowest position and one in the center and preheat the oven to 400°F.

To finish: In a small bowl, whisk together the egg, yogurt, and flour. Brush the surface of each dough round with the egg mixture. Using your fingertips, press all the way around the dough 1½ inches in from the edges, pressing about two-thirds to three-quarters of the way down, to create a border. Inside the border, use your fingertips to create a crosshatch pattern: start by creating lines going up and down across the dough, then create lines left to right to form a grid. Sprinkle a mix of the sesame seeds on top.

Fill a large baking dish with hot water and place it on the lowest oven rack to create steam. Bake the bread until golden brown, 15 to 16 minutes.

Remove the bread from the oven and enjoy your freshly baked Turkish bread warm.

THE BEST PIZZA DOUGH

When I started developing my own pizza dough, I kept going back and forth between craving a New York–style crust and a Neapolitan one. But then it hit me—I could have the best of both worlds! This dough gives you that signature New York–style crispy undercarriage with a bit of flop, while also delivering that fluffy, bubbly crust that's so characteristic of Neapolitan pizza. Bonus: You don't need a fancy oven to get great results at home. This recipe makes enough for four pizzas, but if you don't need them all at once, you can freeze the dough—just thaw it at room temperature the day you want to use it.

MAKES ENOUGH FOR FOUR 10- TO 12-INCH PIZZAS

- 1⅔ cups (390g) warm water
- 2 teaspoons sugar
- 1¼ teaspoons instant yeast
- 3¾ cups (525g) bread flour or all-purpose flour
- 2¼ teaspoons salt
- 2 tablespoons olive oil, plus more for the bowl
- Semolina flour, for rolling out

In the bowl of a stand mixer (or a large bowl if making by hand), combine the warm water, sugar, and yeast. Stir until dissolved, then cover and let sit for 10 minutes until foamy.

Add the olive oil, about half of the flour, snap on the dough hook, and mix on medium-low speed until a shaggy dough forms, 1 to 2 minutes. (Or mix with a wooden spoon.)

Sprinkle in the salt, then gradually add the remaining flour. Knead on low speed until smooth and elastic, 6 to 8 minutes (see Tip, page 206). (Or knead the dough by hand on a clean work surface until it is soft and bounces back when poked, 7 to 8 minutes. If the dough is too sticky at first, cover for 15 minutes and then proceed with kneading.)

Transfer the dough to a lightly oiled bowl. If using your stand mixer, you can just pull the dough gently away from the edges of the bowl, add some oil to the bowl, and swirl to coat. Cover tightly with plastic wrap and a clean kitchen towel and let the dough rest for 30 minutes at room temperature.

Perform a set of folds: Grab the dough from one side, pull up, then fold over across the center of the dough mass. Rotate the bowl 90 degrees and repeat. Do this four times total, pulling from each side.

Cover and let the dough rest for 30 minutes, then repeat the pull-and-fold process two more times, waiting 30 minutes after each set of folds.

Cover the bowl and let the dough rest at room temperature until doubled in size, 2 to 3 hours.

The dough is ready to use now (see Making Pizza, page 206). If not using right away, refrigerate the dough for up to 2 days. Or roll into balls of about 8½ ounces each and wrap any portions not being used in plastic wrap. Pop them into a ziplock bag and store in the freezer. Just let it come to room temperature before assembling and baking your pizza.

MAKING PIZZA

Get your toppings ready. As a rule of thumb, for a 10- to 12-inch pizza, use ⅓ to ½ cup sauce, 4 to 5 ounces cheese, ¼ cup veggies, and 1 to 2 ounces meat.

If you haven't already done so, divide the dough into equal portions of about 8½ ounces, shape each portion into a smooth dough ball, and let the balls rest, covered, for 30 minutes to 1 hour.

Place a baking steel on the middle rack of the oven and preheat the oven to 500°F, or as high as it goes, for 45 minutes to 1 hour. If you don't have a baking steel, you can use a pizza stone or even flip a heavy-duty baking sheet upside down and let it preheat—it won't hold heat quite as well, but it still works great.

Lightly flour a pizza peel with semolina flour. Place a dough ball in the center and start pressing from the middle outward, being careful not to touch the edges where the crust will form. Pressing down on the outer rim can deflate the big airy bubbles. Gently stretch the dough into a 10- to 12-inch round, keeping the edges slightly thicker than the center for a nice, puffy crust. Give the peel a few gentle flicks with your wrist to make sure the dough slides around easily before adding your toppings.

Add the sauce, cheese, and any other toppings. Use the pizza peel to transfer to the oven and slide onto the hot baking steel. Bake for 5 to 7 minutes and monitor closely as each oven will differ with timing. It's done when the crust is puffed up and charred in some spots.

Remove, slice, and serve immediately.

MORIBYAN'S TIPS

I brush the rim with heavy cream for extra browning on the crust.

If you are not using the dough right away and plan to cold-ferment in the fridge for 24 to 48 hours, reduce the kneading time in half. Gluten slowly develops as it ferments in the fridge. Kneading is just a faster way to develop more gluten.

ENGLISH MUFFINS

English muffins make the best breakfast sandwiches and homemade are lighter, fluffier, and so much better than store-bought. I spent a long time developing this recipe because I had to do justice to the English muffin breakfast sandwiches my mom used to make for us (naturally, I have high standards). These muffins are fluffy inside with a nice crispiness on the bottom and top, and when you crack them open with a fork, a little steam escapes before revealing all those perfect nooks and crannies. Enjoy them with butter and jam or as the base of your perfect breakfast sandwich!

MAKES 9 OR 10 MUFFINS

1⅔ cups (400g) whole milk, heated to 110°F

1 tablespoon sugar

1½ teaspoons active dry yeast

3¼ cups (455g) bread flour or all-purpose flour

1½ teaspoons salt

2 tablespoons unsalted butter, at room temperature

Neutral oil, as needed

¼ cup cornmeal, for dusting

In a small bowl, whisk together the warm milk, sugar, and yeast. Cover with a towel and let it sit for about 10 minutes until foamy.

In a stand mixer fitted with the dough hook (or in a large bowl if mixing by hand), whisk the bread flour and salt until combined. Add the milk mixture and butter, then mix on low speed until a sticky but manageable dough forms, about 2 minutes. (Or mix by hand with a bowl scraper.) The dough will be a bit sticky. It should cling lightly to the bottom of the bowl but not the sides. This high hydration helps give the muffins big holes.

Lightly oil the inside of the bowl (about ½ tablespoon of neutral oil) and transfer the dough to it. Cover tightly with plastic wrap.

Same-day option: Let the dough rise in a warm place until doubled in size, 2 to 3 hours. If you have more time, you can let it rest longer at room temperature for 4 hours.

Overnight option: Place the covered bowl in the refrigerator for 8 to 12 hours. This slow fermentation develops deeper flavor and creates bigger holes in the muffins. The next day, bring the dough to room temperature before shaping.

To cook: Dust a clean surface with cornmeal. Transfer the dough to the surface and press it down lightly to about ¾ inch thick. Brush the top with neutral oil.

Use a 3-inch round cutter to cut out rounds from the dough. Make sure the bottom is covered with cornmeal. Transfer the rounds to a tray, cover, and proof in a warm place until puffed up, about 45 minutes.

Heat a cast-iron skillet over medium-low heat and lightly oil the surface. Cook the muffins in batches, covered, until deep golden brown on both sides and the muffins spring back when pressed, 5 to 6 minutes per side. You may need to rotate them to ensure even browning.

Let the muffins cool a bit before splitting them open and toasting. Enjoy with butter, jam, or your favorite toppings!

FLOUR TORTILLAS

Flour tortillas have a reputation for being tricky, but I swear, this was the easiest dough I've ever made. I'm very picky with tortillas; I don't like most store-bought ones, which are too papery in my opinion. A good tortilla is almost translucent, a little bit stretchy, and has a nice chew. The true test is to crumple a tortilla in your hands; if you let it go and it unfolds back into its shape without any tears, you're good to go. I'm happy to report this recipe passes! I always make a big batch of them and keep them stacked in the freezer for breakfast burritos, and tacos on the weekends. They taste so much better than anything you can grab from the store!

MAKES TEN 8-INCH TORTILLAS OR EIGHT 9-INCH TORTILLAS

- 2½ cups (350g) all-purpose flour
- 1¼ teaspoons sea salt
- 1 teaspoon baking powder
- 1 cup (240g) hot water
- 5 tablespoons (2½ ounces/70g) unsalted butter, melted
- 2 tablespoons neutral oil, as needed

In a medium bowl, whisk together the flour, sea salt, and baking powder.

In a separate bowl or measuring cup, mix the hot water with the melted butter.

Pour the liquid into the dry ingredients and stir with your hands or a rubber spatula. The dough will look sticky at first, but keep kneading until it comes together. Turn the dough onto a clean surface and knead for about 5 minutes until smooth. Cover with plastic wrap and let rest for 30 minutes.

After resting, divide the dough into 10 equal portions of 60 to 65g each. Roll each into a ball and place on a lightly oiled tray, lightly coating each ball in oil. Cover and let rest again for 30 minutes.

Preheat a large skillet over medium to medium-high heat. Lightly coat it with oil—not to fry, just enough to prevent sticking, about 1½ teaspoons.

On a lightly floured surface with a rolling pin, roll each ball out into a paper-thin round, as thin as you can go—8 to 9 inches in diameter. It should be see-through when you run your fingers underneath.

Transfer to a hot skillet. Cook until air bubbles begin to form, 30 to 60 seconds. Flip and cook the other side until golden bubbles form and puff up, another 30 seconds.

As soon as each tortilla is done, stack it and cover with a clean kitchen towel to keep them warm and soft. Store tortillas in a ziplock bag at room temperature for up to 5 days, or in the fridge for 1 week. To reheat, warm in the microwave for 30 seconds.

CHEESE-STUFFED GARLIC NAAN

If you're new to baking, naan is the perfect place to start. The dough comes together fast—no overnight proofing, no kneading, just simple, soft, pillowy bread. Here, I'm stuffing it with mozzarella, but that's just the beginning. Try it with jalapeños, a combo of cheese *and* jalapeños, or even spiced ground beef. Whenever I make Creamy Butter Chicken (page 132), a side of cheesy naan isn't just optional, it's mandatory.

MAKES SIX 9-INCH NAAN

GARLIC BUTTER

4 tablespoons (2 ounces/55g) unsalted butter, melted
2 teaspoons minced garlic
⅛ teaspoon salt, or more to taste
1 tablespoon chopped fresh cilantro

DOUGH

1 cup (240g) warm water
2 teaspoons sugar
2 teaspoons active dry yeast
3 cups (420g) all-purpose flour, plus more if needed
¼ cup (60g) whole-milk plain yogurt
3 tablespoons unsalted butter, melted
1½ teaspoons salt

TO FINISH

1½ cups shredded mozzarella cheese
Vegetable oil or ghee, for cooking the naan

Make the garlic butter: In a small bowl, mix the melted butter, garlic, salt, and cilantro. Set aside.

Make the dough: In the bowl of a stand mixer (or in a large bowl if mixing by hand), mix together the warm water, sugar, and yeast. Cover and let it sit until foamy, about 10 minutes.

Add the flour, yogurt, melted butter, and salt to the yeast mixture. Snap on the dough hook and mix on low speed until a dough forms, 2 to 3 minutes. If the dough is too sticky to handle, add 1 to 3 tablespoons more flour. (Or, if working by hand, use a spoon or your hands to mix until the dough begins to come together. Once it does, transfer the dough to a lightly floured surface and knead until it's smooth and elastic, 5 to 7 minutes.)

Cover and let the dough rest in a warm place until doubled in size, about 1 hour.

To finish: Divide the dough into 6 equal portions and roll each piece into a disc. Flatten each piece a little to be slightly larger than the palm of your hand and place 3 to 4 tablespoons shredded mozzarella in the center.

Fold the edges of the dough over the cheese, sealing it tightly, then gently roll it out into a round about ¼ inch thick.

Heat a cast-iron skillet over medium heat and lightly coat it with vegetable oil or ghee. Working in batches, cook each naan until golden brown and puffed up, 2 to 3 minutes per side.

Brush the hot naan with the garlic butter as soon as it comes off the pan. Serve warm and enjoy!

MELT-IN-YOUR-MOUTH BISCUITS

I used to think all biscuits were dry, crumbly, and honestly not worth the hype until I had a Chick-fil-A biscuit. One bite in and I was hooked—so I went deep into research mode, watching behind-the-scenes videos of Chick-fil-A employees making them, to figure out how to do it at home.

Freezing the butter and grating it helps it distribute evenly without it melting, creating those perfect flaky layers. A mix of baking powder and baking soda gives them lift, browning, and just enough spread. When cutting, press straight down, no twisting! Twisting seals the edges and keeps them from rising. And for that rich, golden finish, brush with melted butter the second they come out of the oven.

MAKES 12 BISCUITS

- 2 cups (280g) all-purpose flour, plus more for dusting
- 2 tablespoons cornstarch
- 2 tablespoons sugar
- 1½ tablespoons baking powder
- 1 teaspoon salt
- ¼ teaspoon baking soda
- 12 tablespoons (6 ounces/170g) unsalted butter, frozen for 30 minutes
- 1¼ cups (290g) cold buttermilk
- 3 tablespoons unsalted butter, melted, for brushing

Preheat the oven to 425°F.

In a large bowl, whisk together the flour, cornstarch, sugar, baking powder, salt, and baking soda until well combined.

Using the large holes of a box grater, grate the frozen butter into the dry ingredients and gently toss to combine evenly.

Pour the cold buttermilk into the flour mixture and stir gently with a fork or spatula until a soft dough forms. Be careful not to overmix. It will be a sticky dough!

Sprinkle flour on a clean work surface and place the dough on top. Sprinkle flour on top. Gently pat it into a 1-inch-thick rectangle.

With a short side facing you, fold the short ends of the dough inward to make three overlapping layers (like folding a letter). Then rotate the dough 90 degrees. You will have a short side facing you again, so repeat the process of folding the ends inward to make three layers again.

Pat the dough out into a 1-inch-thick rectangle again. Use a 3-inch round biscuit cutter to cut out 12 biscuits. When you're cutting the biscuits, do not twist the cutter, just press down. Re-roll the scraps as needed to cut out more but do your best not to overwork the dough.

Lightly butter a nonstick baking sheet. Arrange the biscuits on the prepared baking sheet, very close together but not touching, ¼ to ½ inch apart.

Bake until the tops are golden brown, 12 to 13 minutes.

As soon as the biscuits come out of the oven, brush the tops with melted butter. Allow the biscuits to cool slightly on the baking sheet before serving warm.

FLAKY SCALLION PARATHAS

So many cultures have their own version of buttery, flaky, pan-fried flatbreads. In Morocco, we have msemmen; in South and Southeast Asia, there's roti and paratha. Growing up, my mom always kept paratha stocked in the freezer, and from a young age, I remember frying them up myself to enjoy as an afterschool snack.

Making paratha from scratch is incredibly rewarding and surprisingly simple since it's an unleavened bread. My number one tip? Don't be shy with the oil, butter, or ghee! You need a generous amount—both spread between the layers of dough and when frying the paratha. If you've ever watched grandmas making them, you'll see butter or ghee everywhere. The more you use, the better the flaky layers and buttery goodness you'll get.

MAKES 8 PARATHAS

- 4 cups (560g) all-purpose flour
- 2 teaspoons salt
- 1½ cups (355g) warm water
- 1 large egg
- 2 tablespoons unsalted butter, melted
- 2 tablespoons ghee, for coating dough

In a large bowl, whisk together the flour and salt.

In a liquid measuring cup, combine the warm water, egg, and melted butter. Whisk together until homogeneous. Add the wet ingredients to the dry, then, with a wooden spoon, mix everything until it starts coming together into a shaggy dough.

Transfer to a clean work surface and knead with your hands until it just comes together, about 2 minutes. Do not overknead.

Wrap the dough in plastic and let it rest for 30 minutes. Quickly knead it again to form a smooth round ball.

Divide the dough into 8 equal pieces. Coat each piece generously with ghee, place them on a plate or tray, cover with plastic wrap, and refrigerate for 6 to 8 hours.

RECIPE & INGREDIENTS CONTINUE

To assemble: Remove the dough from the fridge 1 hour before rolling to bring to room temperature.

Generously oil a large, clean surface and place one dough piece on it.

Start gently stretching the dough into a round by picking up the ends and pulling on it slowly. The dough should be very stretchy without tearing. Continue gently stretching until it becomes paper-thin and see-through.

Sprinkle about ¼ cup of chopped green onions on the top of the dough round. Roll the dough loosely into a cylinder from one end to the other to seal the green onions in there.

Using one end of the dough cylinder as your middle point, wrap the dough cylinder into a spiral. Tuck the end of the dough cylinder underneath. Repeat with the remaining dough.

Cover and let the spiraled dough rest for 15 minutes.

Using a rolling pin, flatten each swirl onto parchment paper, ⅛ to ¼ inch thick and 8 inches wide, stacking them on a plate, in between layers of parchment, as you go.

Preheat a skillet over medium heat until hot. Add ghee to the pan—figure about 1 tablespoon per paratha.

Once the oil is hot, place a paratha in the pan and cook until the bottom is golden brown, 2 to 3 minutes. Flip and cook the other side for another 2 to 3 minutes, pressing down lightly for even browning.

Repeat with the remaining paratha, then serve warm.

ASSEMBLY

¼ cup neutral oil, for spreading and shaping

1 to 1½ cups finely chopped green onions

Ghee or vegetable oil, for frying

PILLOWY BAO BUNS

I love to bake, and even I'll admit that dough recipes can be tricky. But not this one! Whereas many of the dough recipes in this book are the result of lots of trial and error, this is the first one I got right on the first try. Think of bao as dough that is steamed instead of baked. They are soft, fluffy, and slightly chewy, with a mild, neutral flavor that makes the perfect canvas for bold fillings. Biting into one is like biting into a cloud.

There are so many ways to use these buns. One of my favorites is to stuff them with Dynamite Shrimp (page 81). But you could also use them to repurpose leftover Chinese takeout—bao stuffed with Peking duck or orange chicken would be heavenly. The sky's the limit!

MAKES 14 TO 16 BUNS

- 2⅓ cups (325g) all-purpose flour
- 2 tablespoons sugar
- 2 teaspoons instant yeast
- 1 teaspoon salt
- ½ teaspoon baking powder
- 1 cup (240g) lukewarm milk
- 3 tablespoons vegetable oil

In a stand mixer fitted with the dough hook (or in a large bowl if mixing by hand), mix together the flour, sugar, yeast, salt, and baking powder.

Add the milk and 2 tablespoons of the oil and mix on low speed until a rough dough forms, about 2 minutes. (Or do this by hand with a rubber spatula.)

Mix on medium speed until smooth, soft, and the dough bounces back when pressed, 4 to 5 minutes. It shouldn't be dry or sticky; just soft. (Or knead by hand for 5 to 6 minutes.) Lightly grease a large bowl with ½ tablespoon of the oil and place the dough inside. Cover tightly with plastic wrap and let it rest in a warm spot until more than doubled in size, about 1½ hours.

Punch down the dough, and on a clean work surface, roll it out to about ¼ inch thick.

Use a 3- to 3½-inch round cutter (or a cup) to cut out rounds; you should get 14 to 16. (You can reroll the scraps once and cut again.) Lightly brush each round with the remaining ½ tablespoon oil, then fold them over to create a half-moon shape. Press down gently, just enough so it holds its fold while steaming, but not so much that the edges seal shut.

RECIPE CONTINUES

Line a steamer with a perforated parchment paper round (the kind with holes for steam to circulate). If you don't have those, cut out 14 to 16 individual parchment squares, each about 3½ inches. Place each bun on a parchment square if using.

Cover and let the shaped buns rest for 30 minutes while bringing a pot of water fitted with a steaming rack to a boil.

Working in batches, arrange as many buns 2 inches apart (on the parchment squares or directly on the perforated parchment round) as can comfortably fit in your steamer.

Cover the steamer and steam for 8 minutes. Then, crack open the lid slightly and continue steaming for another 2 minutes. If done, they should be bouncy and spring back when poked!

Serve warm with your favorite fillings.

MORIBYAN'S TIP

If you steam and cool your bao, then store them in an airtight container (or ziplock bag) with a paper towel to absorb moisture, they will keep at room temperature for up to 1 day.

BURGER BRIOCHE BUNS

There's something so satisfying about making a burger from scratch start to finish, and yes, that includes the bun. It might sound extra, but trust me—once you try homemade brioche, there's no going back. It's soft and pillowy and has that perfect buttery bounce when you give it a little squeeze. And the smell while it's baking? Pure magic.

MAKES 12 BUNS

- 1¼ cups (300g) warm whole milk
- 3 tablespoons sugar
- 2 teaspoons instant yeast
- 3¼ cups (455g) bread flour
- 1½ teaspoons salt
- 1 large egg
- 4 tablespoons (2 ounces/55g) unsalted butter, at room temperature, plus more for the bowl
- Egg wash: 1 large egg beaten with 1 tablespoon whole milk
- Sesame seeds (optional), for topping

In the bowl of a stand mixer (or in a large bowl if mixing by hand), combine the warm milk, sugar, and yeast and stir until dissolved. Cover and let it sit for about 10 minutes until slightly foamy.

Add the flour, salt, and egg to the yeast mixture. Snap on the dough hook and mix on low speed until the dough starts to come together, about 1 minute. Add the softened butter and continue mixing until fully incorporated, about 1 minute more. Knead on low speed until the dough is smooth and elastic, 6 to 8 minutes. (Or use a spoon or your hands to mix until the dough begins to come together. Once it does, transfer the dough to a clean surface and knead until it's smooth and elastic, 8 to 10 minutes.)

Transfer the dough to a lightly buttered bowl, cover, and let it rise in a warm place until doubled in size, about 1½ hours.

Divide the dough into 12 equal portions of 80g each. Roll each portion into a smooth tight ball. Arrange the shaped buns on a baking pan lined with parchment paper, leaving space between them. Flatten each one just slightly so they're flat, not domed on top. Cover and let them proof in a warm place until extra puffy, for 1 to 1½ hours.

Adjust one rack in the lowest position and another in the center and preheat the oven to 375°F. To create steam, place a small baking dish with hot water on the bottom oven rack.

Brush the tops of the buns with the egg wash and sprinkle with sesame seeds (if using).

Bake on the middle rack for 15 minutes, or until golden brown on top.

Let the buns cool slightly on a wire rack before using. Enjoy with your favorite burgers or sandwiches!

PITA POCKETS

Growing up, pita or Arabi bread was on the dinner table for every meal from breakfast to dinner. We always had bags around, and like most Arab kids, my siblings and I would come up with all kinds of wild ideas for what to pair it with. Peanut butter and Marshmallow Fluff was a go-to. We'd even make our own pizza using pita as the base, just spread on some sauce, add cheese, and throw on whatever toppings we had.

The first time I had freshly baked pita at a restaurant, I was blown away. It was thick, soft, and pillowy, so different from the thinner ones we always bought at the store. And I have a strong feeling that once you try making it at home, you'll never go back to the store-bought stuff.

MAKES 6 PITAS

- 1¼ cups (300g) warm water
- 2 teaspoons active dry yeast
- 1 teaspoon sugar
- 3 cups (420g) all-purpose flour, plus more for dusting
- 3 tablespoons olive oil, plus more for the bowl
- 1½ teaspoons salt

In the bowl of a stand mixer (or in a large bowl if mixing by hand), combine the warm water, yeast, and sugar. Cover and let it sit for 10 minutes until foamy.

Add the flour, olive oil, and salt. Snap on the dough hook and mix until a shaggy dough forms, about 1 minute. Then knead the dough until smooth and slightly sticky, 2 to 3 minutes. If working by hand, in a large bowl with a wooden spoon, stir everything together until a shaggy dough forms. Turn it out onto a lightly floured surface and knead until smooth and slightly sticky, 5 to 6 minutes.

Transfer the dough to a lightly oiled bowl, coat with olive oil, cover, and let it rise in a warm place until doubled in size, about 2 hours.

Preheat the oven to 500°F and place a sheet pan, pizza stone, cast-iron skillet, or baking steel inside to heat up.

Divide the dough into 6 equal portions and shape into round smooth balls. Place them on a clean work surface, dust them with flour, cover, and let them rest for 15 to 20 minutes.

Lightly flour a work surface and use a rolling pin to gently roll each dough ball into a thin round ¼ to ½ inch thick. Make sure not to press down too much as you roll out the dough. If desired, you can let the pita rest for 10 to 15 minutes longer, so the gluten relaxes and you have a better chance at nailing that pocket!

Flip each pita over and use your hands or a pizza peel to slide as many as will fit onto the hot pan, stone, or steel. Bake until puffed up and slightly golden on top, 3 to 5 minutes.

Let cool for 10 minutes before slicing open and filling with your favorite ingredients!

BUBBLY FOCACCIA

My dad might just be the world's biggest bread enthusiast, and whenever I visit, I always bake him a fresh loaf of this focaccia.

When it comes out of the oven, the focaccia has a tender, airy interior with a crisp, golden crust and a bounce that makes you want to squeeze it. Cut it into small squares and dip it in olive oil for the simplest snack, or slice larger pieces in half to create the most amazing sandwich. Once you've had a sandwich on homemade focaccia, store-bought will never compare.

SERVES 8

- 1¾ cups (415g) lukewarm water
- 2 teaspoons sugar
- 1½ teaspoons instant yeast
- 3¾ cups (525g) bread flour or all-purpose flour
- 2 teaspoons salt
- 7 tablespoons olive oil, plus more as needed
- Flaky sea salt, for finishing

In the bowl of a stand mixer (or in a large bowl if mixing by hand), combine the warm water, sugar, and yeast. Cover and let it sit for about 10 minutes until the top is bubbly and foamy.

Add the flour and salt. Snap on the dough hook and mix on low speed until soft and elastic, 2 to 3 minutes. (Or mix with a wooden spoon.) The dough will be very sticky. This is completely normal. Focaccia is a high-hydration dough.

To a clean large bowl, add 2 tablespoons of the olive oil. Transfer the dough to the bowl, cover, and let rest for 30 minutes in a warm place.

Do a series of stretches and folds: Start by wetting your hands with water a little so the dough doesn't stick. Reach into the center of the dough, gently lift it up, and let the sides naturally fall and hang down. Then fold those loose sides under the center. Turn the bowl slightly and do it again. Lift from the center, let it stretch and drape, and fold it back in. Do this a total of three times, rotating the bowl each time. Let rest for 30 minutes.

Do three more sets of stretches and folds every 30 minutes (so, four total over the course of 2 hours), keeping it covered in between. After the last set, cover the bowl tightly and refrigerate overnight, 12 to 24 hours.

The next day, coat a 9 × 13-inch baking pan with a good amount of olive oil, about 3 tablespoons. Gently transfer the dough to the pan.

Cover tightly and proof at room temperature until super puffy and bubbly, about 4 hours. It should jiggle when you shake the tray.

Preheat the oven to 450°F.

Drizzle 2 more tablespoons of olive oil on top and dimple the dough all over with your fingers, going all the way down to the bottom without deflating it. Sprinkle it with flaky salt.

Bake until the focaccia is deeply golden on top and crisp around the edges, 20 to 25 minutes.

Let it cool slightly before slicing. Store it in an airtight container at room temp for 2 days, in the fridge for 5 days, or in the freezer for 3 months.

SWEET TREATS

BROWN BUTTER CHOCOLATE CHIP COOKIES

My brown butter chocolate chip cookies are hands down the most popular recipe on my blog, so of course I had to bring them into the cookbook. I took all your feedback and used it to make them even better with just a few tweaks to the method to make sure they come out perfect every time. Don't worry, if you're a fan of the original, this version still has everything you love: thin and crinkly, crispy edges, slightly underbaked centers, and that rich, deep flavor from brown butter and brown sugar. For the chocolate, I swear by the ultimate combo: a mix of milk chocolate chips and semisweet wafers. When you break the cookie in half, you get tantalizing pools of chocolate. Imagine a cheese pull, but with gooey chocolate instead!

MAKES 12 COOKIES

- 16 tablespoons (8 ounces/230g) unsalted butter
- 1¼ cups packed (275g) light or dark brown sugar
- ½ cup (100g) granulated sugar
- 2 tablespoons heavy cream
- 2 large eggs
- 2 teaspoons vanilla extract
- 2¼ cups (315g) all-purpose flour
- 1 teaspoon baking soda
- ½ teaspoon salt
- ⅔ cup (115g) milk chocolate chips or chunks, plus more for topping
- ⅔ cup (115g) semisweet chocolate wafers, plus more for topping

Preheat the oven to 350°F. Line a baking sheet with parchment paper.

In a saucepan, melt the butter over medium heat, stirring with a silicone spatula the entire time. First it will melt, then foam, and then start turning golden with little brown bits forming at the bottom. Keep stirring! After 5 to 8 minutes, once it smells nutty and toasty, remove it from the heat and pour it into a large bowl. Let it cool until it is no longer hot, 10 to 15 minutes.

Add the brown sugar, granulated sugar, and heavy cream to the butter and whisk together until smooth. Add the eggs and vanilla and keep whisking until the mixture is lighter in color and the sugar has mostly dissolved, 2 to 3 minutes. That's what gives the cookies that chewy texture we love.

In a separate bowl, whisk together the flour, baking soda, and salt. Add the dry mix to the wet and stir with a rubber spatula until just combined. Fold in the milk chocolate and semisweet chocolate.

Using a 2-inch cookie scooper, portion out the dough directly onto the prepared baking sheet, spacing about 6 cookies per sheet so they don't spread into each other. Press an extra piece or two of chocolate wafer and/or chunk right on top of each dough ball.

Bake for 9 to 10 minutes, until the edges are crispy and golden and the centers are still soft, ooey, and gooey.

Let them sit on the baking sheet for a few minutes before transferring to a wire rack to cool more. Repeat with the remaining dough until all your cookies are baked. Serve warm, or store them in an airtight container at room temperature for up to 3 days if they even last that long.

OATMEAL CREME PIES

If you're like me and always looked forward to the days when your mom tucked Little Debbie oatmeal creme pies into your lunchbox, this copycat recipe will take you right back to those nostalgic moments. The cookie portion of the pies are packed with the warm, comforting flavor of brown sugar and molasses, with just the right amount of chewiness from the oats. They're thin but perfectly chewy, with a slight crisp around the edges. And the creme filling? Marshmallow Fluff gives it that classic stretchy, pull-apart effect for the ultimate nostalgic bite. It took me over fifteen tries to get these just right, and honestly, they taste way better than the packaged version and are a more appropriate size for an adult.

MAKES 12 PIES

- 1¾ cups (245g) all-purpose flour
- 1 cup (90g) quick oats
- 2 teaspoons baking soda
- 1 teaspoon ground cinnamon
- ½ teaspoon salt
- 12 tablespoons (6 ounces/170g) unsalted butter, at room temperature
- ⅓ cup (70g) light brown sugar
- ⅔ cup (135g) granulated sugar, plus more for rolling
- ¼ cup (80g) molasses
- 1 large egg
- 1½ teaspoons vanilla extract

CREME FILLING

- 8 tablespoons (4 ounces/115g) unsalted butter, at room temperature
- 1 cup Marshmallow Fluff
- ⅓ cup powdered sugar
- 1 teaspoon vanilla extract

Preheat the oven to 350°F. Line a baking sheet with parchment paper.

In a medium bowl, whisk together the flour, oats, baking soda, cinnamon, and salt. Set aside.

In a stand mixer fitted with the paddle, beat the butter, brown sugar, and granulated sugar on medium speed until light and fluffy, 1 to 2 minutes.

Mix in the molasses, egg, and vanilla, beating until well combined.

Add the dry ingredients to the wet ingredients and mix on low speed until just combined.

Using a 1.5-inch cookie scoop, portion out the dough and roll each ball in some granulated sugar. Arrange on the prepared baking sheet about 2 inches apart.

Bake until the edges are golden and crispy, 8 to 10 minutes.

Take out of the oven and bang the pan on the counter to help the cookies deflate. Let cool on the baking sheet for a few minutes before transferring them to a wire rack to cool completely.

Make the creme filling: In a stand mixer fitted with the paddle, beat the butter on medium speed until smooth and creamy, 2 to 3 minutes.

Add the Marshmallow Fluff, powdered sugar, and vanilla and beat until light and fluffy, about 1 minute more.

Once the cookies are completely cool, match them up by size to create even pairs. Pipe or spread a layer of filling onto the flat side of one cookie, then gently press another cookie on top to form a sandwich.

Let the cookies set for a few minutes before serving.

TIRAMISÙ-INSPIRED BROWNIE BARS

This dessert is as beautiful as it is delicious. It starts with a brownie base—my take on the Ghirardelli box mix brownies, which are hard to beat with their shiny, crinkly top and ultra fudgy center. I add a touch of espresso powder to the batter to tie it into the layers that follow. On top of the brownies are coffee-soaked ladyfingers, then a rich and creamy mascarpone filling to finish it off. Once you slice into it, you can see all the distinct layers and it's a total showstopper for something as simple as a brownie!

MAKES 12 OR 16 BROWNIES

BROWNIE LAYER

- 16 tablespoons (8 ounces/225g) unsalted butter
- 1⅓ cups (265g) granulated sugar
- ¼ cup (55g) light brown sugar
- 2 tablespoons vegetable oil
- ½ cup (85g) chopped semisweet chocolate
- ½ cup (50g) Dutch-process cocoa powder
- ½ teaspoon espresso powder
- ½ teaspoon salt
- ½ tablespoon vanilla extract
- 3 large eggs, at room temperature
- 1 large egg yolk, at room temperature
- ⅔ cup (90g) all-purpose flour
- ½ cup (85g) semisweet chocolate chips

MASCARPONE CREAM

- 10 ounces mascarpone
- ½ cup powdered sugar
- 1 cup heavy cream
- 1 teaspoon vanilla extract

ASSEMBLY

- 1 cup strong brewed coffee
- 3 tablespoons brown sugar
- 16 ladyfingers
- ¼ cup cocoa powder, for dusting

Make the brownies: Preheat the oven to 325°F. Line an 8 × 8-inch square baking pan with parchment paper.

In a saucepan, melt the butter over medium heat. Add the granulated sugar, brown sugar, and vegetable oil, whisking until the mixture is smooth and slightly dissolved. Remove from the heat and stir in the chopped chocolate, mixing until fully melted and glossy.

In a medium bowl, whisk together cocoa powder, espresso powder, and salt until combined. Add the melted butter/chocolate mixture and whisk together again until smooth. Set aside to cool slightly.

To the same bowl, stir in the vanilla, then add the whole eggs and egg yolk, one at a time, mixing well after each addition.

In a separate bowl, sift the flour to ensure there are no lumps. Add the flour to the wet ingredients, gently folding until just combined. Do not overmix. Stir in the chocolate chips, then pour the batter into the prepared pan and smooth the top with a spatula.

Bake until a toothpick inserted in the center comes out with a few moist crumbs, 25 to 27 minutes. Let the brownies cool completely in the pan.

Make the mascarpone cream: In a stand mixer fitted with the paddle (or in a large bowl using a hand mixer), combine the mascarpone, powdered sugar, heavy cream, and vanilla. Mix on medium speed to beat everything together until smooth, fluffy, and thick enough to hold its shape, 1 to 2 minutes. (It will start liquidy but don't worry; it'll come together!)

Assemble the brownies: In a shallow bowl, mix the brewed coffee and brown sugar until dissolved. Dip a ladyfinger into the coffee mixture briefly, then place it on top of the cooled brownies. Repeat this process of dipping and arranging the ladyfingers until you have 2 rows of 8. Spread the mascarpone cream evenly over the arranged ladyfingers.

Refrigerate for at least 2 hours to allow the flavors to meld. Finish it off with a dusting of cocoa powder to cover the top. Slice and serve!

ALMOND CROISSANT BROWN BUTTER BLONDIES

These blondies bring together the best of both worlds: the rich, chewy base of a brown butter blondie and the luscious almond filling you love from an almond croissant. The blondie layer is packed with deep brown-butter flavor and plenty of chew, while the almond filling on top tastes just like the center of an almond croissant—nutty and perfectly crisp around the edges. A sprinkling of sliced almonds adds the perfect crunch to finish it off. And if you're craving a chocolate almond croissant twist, fold some chocolate chips into the blondie base for an extra treat!

MAKES 12 BLONDIES

BLONDIE BASE

- 12 tablespoons (6 ounces/170g) unsalted butter
- 1 cup (220g) lightly packed light brown sugar
- ⅓ cup (65g) granulated sugar
- 1 large egg
- 1 large egg yolk
- 1 tablespoon vanilla extract
- 1½ cups (210g) all-purpose flour
- ½ teaspoon salt
- ¼ teaspoon baking powder

FRANGIPANE (ALMOND CREAM FILLING)

- 6 tablespoons (3 ounces/85g) unsalted butter, at room temperature
- ⅓ cup granulated sugar
- ¾ cup almond flour
- ⅛ teaspoon salt
- 1 teaspoon vanilla extract
- ¾ teaspoon almond extract
- 1 large egg

ASSEMBLY

- ⅔ cup sliced almonds
- Powdered sugar, for dusting

Preheat the oven to 350°F. Line an 8 × 8-inch square pan with parchment paper.

Make the blondie base: In a small saucepan, melt the butter over medium heat, stirring constantly. Continue cooking until the butter turns golden brown and smells nutty, 6 to 8 minutes. Remove from the heat and transfer to a large bowl to cool for 10 minutes.

To the brown butter, add the brown sugar and granulated sugar. Whisk together until smooth.

Add the whole egg, egg yolk, and vanilla, whisking until fully incorporated.

In a medium bowl, whisk together the flour, salt, and baking powder. Add the dry ingredients to the wet ingredients and fold with a rubber spatula until a cookie dough forms.

Transfer the blondie dough into the pan, pressing it down evenly with clean hands or a spatula.

Make the frangipane: In a medium bowl with an electric mixer, beat the butter and granulated sugar together until smooth, 1 to 2 minutes. Add the almond flour, salt, vanilla, almond extract, and egg. Mix until creamy and combined.

Assemble the blondies: Use a rubber spatula to spread the frangipane evenly on top of the blondie base, then sprinkle sliced almonds on top.

Bake until golden brown, set in the center, and a toothpick comes out clean, 25 to 30 minutes. Check on it at 15 to 20 minutes; if it's already golden brown on top, tent with foil.

Let cool for 30 minutes to 1 hour before dusting lightly with powdered sugar, then slice and enjoy!

BEST BANANA BREAD

I take banana bread very seriously, even though it might be the most basic thing in the world. There are a million recipes out there, so why should you try mine? The flavor is all about the banana, complemented by a rich depth from the brown sugar, and sour cream makes the bread unbelievably moist and tender. I spent years tweaking ratios and ingredients until I landed on the perfect version. And I know it's good because my mom started overbuying bananas on purpose so that they'd overripen and I'd have to turn them into banana bread.

MAKES 8 SLICES

- 1⅓ cups (185g) all-purpose flour
- 1 teaspoon baking soda
- ½ teaspoon salt
- ¼ teaspoon baking powder
- ¼ teaspoon ground cinnamon
- ½ cup (100g) vegetable oil
- ¾ cup (165g) light brown sugar
- ¼ cup (50g) granulated sugar
- 2 large eggs
- 1½ teaspoons vanilla extract
- 3 overripe bananas, mashed
- ¼ cup (55g) sour cream
- ¾ cup (130g) semisweet chocolate chips

Preheat the oven to 325°F. Line a 9 × 5-inch loaf pan with parchment paper.

In a medium bowl, whisk together the flour, baking soda, salt, baking powder, and cinnamon. Set aside.

In a large bowl, whisk together the vegetable oil, light brown sugar, and granulated sugar. Add the eggs one at a time, whisking well after each addition. Stir in the vanilla, mashed bananas, and the sour cream until fully incorporated.

Add the dry ingredients all at once to the wet mixture. Using a rubber spatula, gently fold the mixture together until just combined. Be careful not to overmix.

Gently fold in most of the chocolate chips, reserving a handful for topping.

Pour the batter into the prepared loaf pan. Sprinkle the remaining chocolate chips on top.

Bake until a toothpick inserted into the center comes out clean (a few crumbs are fine, but it shouldn't be wet), 55 to 65 minutes. After 30 minutes, check the bread; if it's already browned on top, loosely cover it with aluminum foil to prevent overbrowning.

Let the banana bread cool in the pan for about 10 minutes. Then, remove it from the pan and allow it to cool completely—at least 1 hour, but the longer it cools, the better the flavor! If desired, you can tent the bread with foil again (after removing it from the pan) for 1 hour or more to keep it extra moist. (This creates the ooey-gooey top.) Once fully cooled, slice and enjoy!

BLUEBERRY CINNAMON CRUNCH COFFEE CAKE

When I first started baking, I always gravitated toward cakes like this one: It's fluffy, moist, and not overly sweet. My goal with this cake was to figure out how to mimic the crumbly, crispy texture of a coffee cake without going through the trouble of making a crumble topping. Turns out, sprinkling brown sugar and cinnamon on the top before baking does the trick. This cake is wonderful alongside Moroccan mint tea, which my family drinks every night. On Friday nights, my dad would meet his friends at a coffee shop and he'd always ask me to whip up this cake so he could take it along to share. That's how I know it's good!

MAKES 12 SLICES

- 2 cups (280g) all-purpose flour, plus 1 tablespoon for the blueberries
- 1 tablespoon cornstarch
- 2 teaspoons baking powder
- ½ teaspoon baking soda
- ½ teaspoon salt
- ⅔ cup (135g) granulated sugar
- ⅔ cup (145g) light brown sugar
- ⅓ cup (65g) vegetable oil
- 5 tablespoons (2½ ounces/70g) unsalted butter, at room temperature
- 2 large eggs, beaten
- ½ cup (115g) whole-milk plain yogurt
- ½ cup (120g) whole milk
- 1½ teaspoons vanilla extract
- 2 cups (300g) blueberries

CINNAMON-SUGAR TOPPING

- ½ cup light brown sugar
- 1 teaspoon ground cinnamon

Preheat the oven to 350°F. Line an 8 × 8-inch square baking pan with parchment paper.

In a medium bowl, whisk together the 2 cups (280g) flour, cornstarch, baking powder, baking soda, and salt.

In a large bowl, using an electric mixer, beat together the granulated sugar, brown sugar, oil, and butter until smooth and creamy, 3 to 4 minutes. Add the eggs, yogurt, milk, and vanilla and beat together until well combined, about 1 minute.

Add the dry ingredients to the wet ingredients and beat together one last time until just combined.

In a small bowl, toss the blueberries with the remaining 1 tablespoon flour until they are lightly coated. This helps prevent them from sinking in the batter. Use a spatula to gently fold in the coated blueberries.

Make the cinnamon-sugar topping: In a small bowl, mix together the brown sugar and cinnamon.

Pour the batter into the prepared pan and sprinkle the cinnamon/sugar mixture evenly over the top. Bake until a toothpick inserted into the center comes out clean, 55 minutes. Check 30 minutes into cooking: If it is browning on top too quickly, loosely cover it with foil.

Allow the cake to cool in the pan for about 30 minutes before cutting into squares and serving.

PISTACHIO OLIVE OIL CAKE

Growing up in an Arab household, olive oil was always a staple in our kitchen. Because of this, Italian olive oil cake has become a favorite in my house. I wanted to take it up a notch by making a pistachio-flavored version, topping it with lightly sweetened ricotta cream, and amplifying the pistachio flavor with a glossy pool of pistachio butter on top. The result is a vibrant green cake with a delicate crumb that's tender, moist, and bursting with pistachio flavor in every bite.

SERVES 8

CAKE

1¼ cups (130g) raw pistachios
1½ cups (210g) all-purpose flour
¾ teaspoon baking powder
½ teaspoon baking soda
½ teaspoon salt
1½ cups (300g) granulated sugar
3 large eggs
1 cup (220g) extra-virgin olive oil
½ cup (120g) whole milk
½ cup (115g) sour cream
1½ teaspoons vanilla extract
½ teaspoon almond extract

FROSTING

½ cup ricotta cheese
½ cup heavy cream
⅓ cup powdered sugar

TO FINISH

⅓ cup pistachio butter
2 tablespoons finely chopped pistachios

Make the cake: Preheat the oven to 350°F. Line a 9-inch round cake pan with a round of parchment paper.

In a food processor or high-powered blender, process the pistachios until they become a powder. Make sure not to overprocess, or you'll end up with pistachio butter. You should have 1 cup of pistachio flour (if for some reason you don't, grind more pistachios!).

In a medium bowl, whisk together the pistachio flour, all-purpose flour, baking powder, baking soda, and salt.

In a large bowl, whisk together the granulated sugar and eggs until pale and slightly thickened, 2 to 3 minutes. Add the olive oil, milk, sour cream, vanilla, and almond extract. Whisk again for another minute, just until smooth and well blended.

Add the dry mixture to the wet ingredients and gently whisk until just combined. Pour the batter into the prepared cake pan.

Bake until a toothpick inserted in the center comes out clean, 45 to 50 minutes. If the top starts to brown too fast, loosely cover it with foil.

Let the cake cool in the pan for 15 minutes, then transfer it to a plate to cool completely before frosting.

Make the frosting: In a medium bowl, with an electric mixer, combine the ricotta, heavy cream, and powdered sugar and mix on medium speed until the frosting is smooth and fluffy and holds its shape.

To finish: Once the cake is fully cooled, spread the frosting all over the top, making sure the outer inch is a bit higher. Pour the pistachio butter in the center and gently spread it to cover the surface. Sprinkle finely chopped pistachios to finish.

COOKIES & CREAM TRES LECHES CAKE

Tres leches is one of my favorite desserts, and I take it VERY seriously. After four years of perfecting my recipe, I'm confident this is the one. One day, I had too many Oreo cookies lying around and decided to add them to the mix. It was fantastic, like cookies and milk in cake form. If you want to add Biscoff cookies instead of Oreos, go for it. Sprinkles? Absolutely! A confetti tres leches sounds heavenly!

MAKES 16 SLICES

CAKE

- 1½ cups (210g) all-purpose flour
- 2 teaspoons baking powder
- ½ teaspoon salt
- 5 large eggs, separated, at room temperature
- 1 cup (200g) granulated sugar
- 2 teaspoons vanilla extract
- ½ cup (120g) whole milk
- 1 cup (100g) crushed Oreos (about 9 cookies)

TRES LECHES SOAKING MIXTURE

- 1 (14-ounce) can sweetened condensed milk
- 1 (12-ounce) can evaporated milk
- ¾ cup half-and-half

FROSTING AND TOPPING

- 1½ cups heavy whipping cream
- ¼ cup powdered sugar, or to taste
- 4 Oreo cookies, crushed

Preheat the oven to 350°F.

Make the cake: In a medium bowl, whisk together the flour, baking powder, and salt. Set aside.

In a large bowl, using an electric mixer, beat the egg yolks, granulated sugar, and vanilla until the mixture is smooth and lighter in color, 2 to 3 minutes. Mix in the milk until fully incorporated, about 1 more minute.

Add the dry ingredients to the wet ingredients and beat together until combined, 1 to 2 minutes.

In a stand mixer fitted with the whisk (or in a bowl using a hand mixer), beat the egg whites to stiff peaks, 5 to 6 minutes. Use a rubber spatula to gently fold the whipped egg whites into the batter in two or three additions, taking care not to deflate the batter. Gently fold in the 1 cup crushed Oreos. Pour the batter into the baking pan and spread evenly.

Bake until a toothpick inserted in the center comes out clean, 20 to 25 minutes. Allow to cool in the pan.

Meanwhile, make the tres leches mixture: In a large bowl, whisk together the sweetened condensed milk, evaporated milk, and half-and-half until fully combined.

Once the cake has cooled completely, use a fork to poke holes all over the surface. It's tedious but poke a lot to ensure there are no dry spots.

Slowly pour the tres leches mixture evenly over the cake, allowing it to soak in. Refrigerate for at least 2 to 3 hours and up to overnight, to fully absorb the liquid.

Make the frosting and topping: In a large bowl, use an electric mixer with the whisk attachment to beat the heavy whipping cream with the powdered sugar until stiff peaks form, 5 to 6 minutes. Spread the whipped cream evenly over the soaked cake, then sprinkle with the crushed Oreos on top. Slice and serve.

PEACH COBBLER

The minute peaches hit the farmers' market, it's officially peach cobbler season. Everything comes together right in the oven, from the peaches softening and caramelizing into a sweet, jammy filling to the golden, buttery topping that bakes up crisp on the edges and tender in the middle. It comes out bubbling and fragrant, practically begging for a scoop of vanilla ice cream on top to melt into every bite.

SERVES 4 TO 6

PEACH FILLING

- 6 ripe peaches (3 to 3½ pounds), peeled and sliced
- ½ cup packed brown sugar
- 3 tablespoons unsalted butter, cut into small cubes
- 1½ tablespoons cornstarch
- 1½ teaspoons fresh lemon juice
- 1½ teaspoons vanilla extract
- ½ teaspoon ground cinnamon
- Pinch of ground nutmeg
- Pinch of salt

COBBLER TOPPING

- 1½ cups (210g) all-purpose flour
- ⅔ cup packed (145g) brown sugar
- 1½ teaspoons baking powder
- ½ teaspoon salt
- 8 tablespoons (4 ounces/115g) unsalted butter, cold
- ½ cup (120g) whole milk
- 1 teaspoon vanilla extract

ASSEMBLY

- 1½ tablespoons turbinado sugar or granulated sugar
- ¼ teaspoon ground cinnamon
- 2 tablespoons heavy cream, for brushing
- Vanilla ice cream, for serving

Preheat the oven to 375°F.

Make the peach filling: Spread the sliced peaches directly into a 9 × 13-inch baking dish. Sprinkle with the brown sugar, butter cubes, cornstarch, lemon juice, vanilla, cinnamon, nutmeg, and salt. Use a spatula or clean hands to gently toss everything together right in the dish until the peaches are evenly coated.

Bake uncovered for 10 minutes to help them release their juices and slightly soften. The riper they are, the less time they'll need in the oven. Don't worry if they're still a bit firm at this point. They'll continue baking once the topping goes on.

Meanwhile, make the cobbler topping: In a bowl, combine the flour, brown sugar, baking powder, and salt. Use the large holes of a box grater to grate the cold butter into the bowl, then use your fingers to work it into the dry mixture until crumbly. Pour in the milk and vanilla, stirring until just combined.

Take the peaches out of the oven and drop spoonfuls of the cobbler topping all over the top. It's okay if some peaches show through. That's what makes it look rustic and beautiful.

Assemble and bake: In a small bowl, stir together the turbinado sugar and the cinnamon. Brush the cobbler topping lightly with heavy cream and sprinkle generously with the cinnamon sugar. Return to the oven.

Bake until golden brown on top and bubbling around the edges, 25 to 30 minutes (I like closer to 30 minutes for an extra golden, crispy topping).

Let it cool slightly before serving. Serve warm with a scoop of vanilla ice cream.

CARROT CAKE STICKY TOFFEE PUDDING

It's hard for me to pick a favorite dessert, but sticky toffee pudding (a.k.a. sticky date cake) definitely makes it into my top five. I first fell in love with it during my trip to England and Scotland, where I couldn't resist ordering it twice a day. Carrot cake also ranks high on my list, so I decided to combine the two. The warm spices of carrot cake and the rich, caramelized brown sugar of sticky toffee pudding complement each other perfectly. This cake is incredibly moist, with all the spice of classic carrot cake, and is drenched in a luscious toffee sauce that ties everything together.

MAKES 12 SLICES

CAKE

- 9 ounces (255g) pitted Medjool dates, chopped
- 1 cup (240g) whole milk
- Oil cooking spray
- 1 teaspoon baking soda
- ⅔ cup (145g) packed dark brown sugar
- 8 tablespoons (4 ounces/115g) unsalted butter, melted
- 2 large eggs, at room temperature
- 1½ teaspoons vanilla extract
- 1½ cups (210g) all-purpose flour
- 1 teaspoon baking powder
- ½ teaspoon salt
- 1 teaspoon ground cinnamon
- ¼ teaspoon ground nutmeg
- ¼ teaspoon ground ginger
- 1 cup (85g) grated carrots, squeezed
- ½ cup (60g) chopped walnuts

TOFFEE SAUCE

- 8 tablespoons (4 ounces/115g) unsalted butter
- ¾ cup heavy cream
- ¾ cup packed dark brown sugar
- Pinch of salt
- ¼ teaspoon ground cinnamon
- 1 teaspoon vanilla extract

Make the cake: Place the dates in a heatproof medium bowl. On the stovetop or in the microwave, bring the milk to a boil and pour over the dates. Stir in the baking soda and let the mixture sit for about 10 minutes until the dates soften. Mash the dates well with a fork or potato masher until they form a thick paste, though some small chunks are fine.

Preheat the oven to 350°F. Grease an 8- or 9-inch square baking pan with cooking spray or line with parchment paper, leaving overhang on the sides for easy lifting.

In a large bowl, whisk together the dark brown sugar and melted butter. Add the date paste, eggs, and vanilla, whisking until smooth.

In a separate bowl, whisk together the flour, baking powder, salt, cinnamon, nutmeg, and ginger.

Add the dry ingredients to the wet ingredients and use a rubber spatula to incorporate until you have a smooth batter.

Fold in the carrots and walnuts and pour the batter into the cake pan.

Bake until a toothpick inserted in the center comes out clean, 25 to 26 minutes.

Meanwhile, make the toffee sauce: In a small saucepan, melt the butter over medium heat. Stir in the heavy cream, dark brown sugar, salt, and cinnamon. Bring to a gentle simmer and cook, stirring frequently, until the sauce thickens, about 5 minutes. Remove from the heat and stir in the vanilla.

Using a skewer or toothpick, poke holes all over the warm cake. Pour two-thirds to three-quarters of the warm toffee sauce over the cake, allowing it to soak in completely. Let it sit for 30 minutes to absorb the flavors.

Cut into slices and serve warm with the remaining toffee sauce drizzled on top of each slice for anyone who wants extra.

BANANA PUDDING CUPS

This fan-favorite recipe from my blog originally started as a copycat of New York City's famous Magnolia Bakery banana pudding. But whenever I'm making a copycat recipe, I always ask myself: *How can I make this even better?* For me, that meant adding a vanilla-cookie crust for a contrast in textures and a little cream cheese in the pudding to cut the sweetness. Just a touch goes a long way.

The great thing about this dessert is you can make it the traditional way, in one large dish, or portion it into single-serve cups, as here. The cups are my favorite when I have friends over because it's easy to send them home with a little treat for later.

SERVES 8 TO 10

CRUST

- 8 ounces (225g) Nilla wafers
- 8 tablespoons (4 ounces/115g) unsalted butter, melted

PUDDING

- 2 cups (480g) cold whole milk
- 1 (5-ounce) package instant vanilla pudding mix
- 1 (14-ounce) can sweetened condensed milk
- 2 ounces cream cheese, at room temperature
- 3 cups (715g) heavy cream
- 1 teaspoon vanilla extract

ASSEMBLY

- 6 large bananas, sliced
- 1 (11-ounce) bag Nilla wafers

Make the crust: In a food processor, process the Nilla wafers until finely ground. Combine 2 cups of the crumbs with the melted butter and mix until evenly combined.

Make the pudding: In a large bowl, whisk together the milk and instant pudding mix until dissolved, 1 to 2 minutes. Let it sit for 10 minutes to thicken, then add the sweetened condensed milk and cream cheese. Whisk vigorously (or use electric beaters) until smooth and creamy. Set aside.

In a medium bowl, using an electric mixer, beat the heavy cream and vanilla until stiff peaks form, 3 to 5 minutes. Be careful not to overwhip.

Gently fold the whipped cream into the pudding mixture using a rubber spatula until fully combined.

In 8 to 10 serving cups (if your cups are around 8 ounces, you'll get 8 servings; if they're smaller, you should get 10), start layering in the following order: crust layer at the bottom, sliced bananas, whole Nilla wafers, and a thick layer of pudding. Repeat the layering sequence once more. Typically, two full layers fill most standard serving containers.

Refrigerate for at least 6 hours to allow the pudding to set and the wafers to soften.

Just before serving, garnish each portion with a banana slice, a Nilla wafer, and a sprinkle of crushed wafers on top.

CLASSIC CRÈME BRÛLÉE

Crème brûlée might look and sound like a fancy, showstopping dessert, and it absolutely is, but it's secretly one of the easiest things to make. It uses just a handful of basic ingredients, comes together with minimal effort, and delivers that perfect contrast of silky custard and crackly caramelized sugar on top. Added bonus: It's surprisingly fun to whip out a blowtorch in the kitchen!

SERVES 6

- 2¼ cups (540g) heavy cream
- 1 tablespoon vanilla bean paste or 1 vanilla bean pod, split and scraped
- 5 egg yolks
- ½ cup (100g) plus 1½ tablespoons sugar
- ⅛ teaspoon salt

Preheat the oven to 300°F.

In a saucepan, warm the heavy cream with the vanilla bean paste over medium heat until it's steaming. Don't let it boil.

In a separate bowl, whisk together the egg yolks, ½ cup (100g) of the sugar, and the salt until pale in color and smooth. Do not overmix or create too many bubbles.

Slowly drizzle a small amount of the warm cream mixture into the yolks, whisking the entire time. Continue whisking as you gradually incorporate the rest of the cream, allowing the yolks to gently adjust to the heat.

Set six 4-ounce ramekins in a baking dish. Fill the baking dish with hot water until it comes halfway up the sides of the ramekins. Then carefully pour the custard mixture into the ramekins.

Bake for 35 to 40 minutes, checking at the 35-minute mark. The custard should be set around the edges but still have a slight jiggle in the center. It's better to slightly underbake than overbake.

Let the ramekins cool to room temperature, then refrigerate for 2 to 4 hours, or overnight.

Sprinkle the remaining sugar evenly over each ramekin (about ¾ teaspoon per ramekin), gently tapping the ramekin to spread it out. Place the ramekins on a baking sheet and broil on high for 3 to 4 minutes, watching closely so the sugar doesn't burn. (Alternatively, use a mini torch to caramelize the sugar until it's golden and crisp.)

Crack through the crust and enjoy!

MORIBYAN'S TIP

To avoid air bubbles in your custard, when you first beat the eggs, do not overmix. After filling the ramekins, lightly tap them on your countertop to allow any bubbles to pop.

WHITE CHOCOLATE RASPBERRY CHEESECAKE

For the longest time, I didn't like cheesecake . . . until I tried the white chocolate and raspberry cheesecake from the Cheesecake Factory. It was tangy, but not *too* tangy thanks to the white chocolate. I immediately knew I had to re-create it at home. I think I tested this three times in a single week because I wanted my cake to be as creamy as the Cheesecake Factory's. (Not to brag, but I think I nailed it.) This is a great dessert to make a day or two in advance, since it holds so well in the fridge. Or, you could make it weeks in advance, wrap it tightly in plastic, and freeze it. When you're ready to serve, thaw at room temperature, and it'll taste as good as fresh.

MAKES ONE 9-INCH CHEESECAKE TO SERVE 8 TO 12

RASPBERRY SAUCE

12 ounces fresh or frozen raspberries
¼ cup sugar
2 teaspoons cornstarch

CRUST

30 Oreo cookies (345g)
5 tablespoons (2½ ounces/70g) unsalted butter, melted

Make the raspberry sauce: In a saucepan, stir together the frozen raspberries, sugar, cornstarch, and ¼ cup (60g) water. Bring to a simmer over medium heat. Use a spoon or spatula to gently mash the berries as they cook for a smoother texture and to extract as much raspberry flavor as possible. Cook until the sauce thickens enough to coat the back of a spoon, 3 to 4 minutes. Strain through a fine-mesh sieve to remove the seeds, then set aside to cool completely.

Adjust a rack to the lowest position and preheat the oven to 325°F.

Make the crust: Line the bottom of a 9-inch springform pan with parchment paper. Wrap the outside of the springform pan with two layers of extra-wide foil (ideally 18 inches wide) to prevent leaks.

In a food processor, blitz the cookies until they resemble very fine sand. Transfer to a medium bowl, then pour in the melted butter and mix until evenly combined.

Press the mixture firmly into the bottom of the prepared pan, making sure the crust goes all the way up the sides and is tightly packed. Using the bottom of a measuring cup can help press it in evenly and get clean edges.

RECIPE & INGREDIENTS CONTINUE

Make the cheesecake batter: In a stand mixer fitted with the paddle (or in a large bowl using a hand mixer), beat the cream cheese, sour cream, and sugar on medium-low speed until smooth and creamy, about 1 minute. Scrape the sides of the bowl with a rubber spatula.

With the mixer on low speed to avoid overmixing, add the eggs one at a time, scraping the sides of the bowl with a rubber spatula in between additions.

Mix in the vanilla and salt until combined.

In a microwave-safe bowl, combine the white chocolate and heavy cream. Roughly mix together and microwave on low power in 20-second increments, stirring after each, until melted and smooth.

With the mixer running on low speed, pour in the melted white chocolate mixture and mix until just combined.

Pour half of the cheesecake batter over the crust. Drizzle ¼ cup of the raspberry sauce over the batter and gently swirl with a knife to create an attractive marbled pattern.

Add the remaining cheesecake batter and smooth the top with a spatula. Drizzle another ¼ cup of raspberry sauce on top and swirl again.

Place the pan inside a larger roasting pan and carefully pour boiling water into the roasting pan until it reaches halfway up the sides of the cheesecake pan.

Bake on the lowest rack until the edges are set but the center still has a little jiggle, 1 hour 10 minutes to 1 hour 20 minutes.

Turn off the oven, crack the door slightly, and let the cheesecake cool in the oven for 1 hour.

Remove from the water bath and let it cool at room temperature for another hour.

Cover and refrigerate for at least 8 hours, preferably overnight. Once fully chilled, remove from the pan and slice.

Drizzle the remaining raspberry sauce over each slice before serving.

MORIBYAN'S TIP

If your oven tends to brown things more than you like, wrap a rack completely in foil and slide it into the highest position of your oven. This should help prevent the top of the cheesecake from browning too much.

CHEESECAKE BATTER

4 (8-ounce/225g) packages cream cheese, at room temperature
⅓ cup (75g) sour cream, at room temperature
¾ cup (150g) sugar
4 large eggs, at room temperature
2 teaspoons vanilla extract
Pinch of salt
2⅔ cups (440g) white chocolate chips
⅔ cup (150g) heavy cream

NO-CHURN FLUFFERNUTTER ICE CREAM

Let me introduce you to a no-churn ice cream that's as easy to prepare as it is to eat! The secret ingredient here is sweetened condensed milk, which gives the ice cream its ultra creamy texture. When I was a kid, my sister introduced me to the combo of peanut butter and Marshmallow Fluff (a.k.a. fluffernutter), which I've loved ever since. We used to have it wrapped in toasted pita, and I loved every bite. Naturally, I had to turn that after-school snack into a no-churn ice cream.

Feel free to customize this recipe however you like. If fluffernutter isn't your thing, try fruit jam, cookie dough, or chocolate brownie chunks. It has the same creamy texture and flavor as store-bought ice cream but it's even better because it's homemade. It takes just 10 minutes to make, then let the freezer do the hard work!

SERVES 4 TO 6

- 2½ cups heavy cream
- 1½ teaspoons vanilla extract
- ⅛ teaspoon salt
- 1 (14-ounce) can sweetened condensed milk
- ½ cup peanut butter
- ½ cup Marshmallow Fluff

In a large bowl, with an electric mixer, beat the heavy cream, vanilla, and salt until it just holds its shape, 2 to 3 minutes. Don't overmix or whip it to very stiff peaks; otherwise, the ice cream won't freeze to the right texture.

Add the sweetened condensed milk and use a rubber spatula to gently fold, keeping the mixture light and airy, until combined and smooth.

Pour half of the mixture into an 8 × 8-inch square pan. Dollop 4 tablespoons each of the peanut butter and Marshmallow Fluff across the surface and gently swirl to create ribbons. Repeat with the remaining ice cream mixture, then add the rest of the peanut butter and Fluff on top. Swirl again to distribute throughout.

Cover the pan with plastic wrap, making sure it touches the surface of the ice cream to prevent ice crystals from forming. Freeze until fully set, at least 6 hours. If the ice cream is too firm to scoop straight from the freezer, let it sit at room temperature for a few minutes before serving.

ACKNOWLEDGMENTS

To my mother and father, thank you for inspiring me not only in the kitchen, but in every part of life. From buying me my first camera and cookbooks to bringing home props and offering recipe ideas, you always nurtured my curiosity and creativity. You supported my passion long before it became a career. What began as a small hobby blossomed into something much bigger because you believed in me. I owe everything to your love, guidance, and unwavering faith.

To my husband, I'm endlessly grateful for your constant love and encouragement and for believing in my dream before I ever did. You've been the best taste tester for this cookbook, my sounding board for ideas big and small, and my steady voice of reassurance whenever I felt overwhelmed. You remind me of my worth on the hardest days and have helped me build the confidence to keep going.

To my siblings, thank you for supporting my dreams from the days of small bake sales to now writing a cookbook. You spent countless nights helping me bake cupcakes and proudly told your friends and coworkers about my blog, always cheering me on in ways big and small. My life is so much brighter with you four in it.

To my mother-in-law, thank you for always showing me so much love and support over the years. You have a gift for making food that feels like care served on a plate and it always brought me comfort in moments I needed it most. Being able to include two of your recipes here is really special.

To my manager, Alicia, and the GCA team, thank you for making this cookbook dream a reality. From handling the behind-the-scenes details like contracts to timelines, you've helped me every step of the way with so much care. Thank you for your hard work, kindness, and belief in me.

To Emily Timberlake, thank you for managing this project with such diligence, and most importantly, love. Your expertise was invaluable in guiding me through writing my first cookbook, and you made the entire process truly filled with warmth. You helped bring the stories behind each recipe to life and ensured every page was clear and easy to follow for readers.

To photographer Eva Kolenko, food stylist Natalie Drobny, food stylist assistant Paige Arnett, and prop stylist Genesis Vallejo, thank you for pouring so much heart and talent into every shot. You brought these recipes to life, capturing the feeling and soul of this book so beautifully. I'm so thankful for the energy and magic you each brought.

To editor, Susan Roxborough, thank you for your thoughtful editorial input and perspective throughout the journey to make this book stronger. I appreciate the time you dedicated to reading and reviewing these pages, and the care you brought to each stage of the process to make this book what it is.

To designer, Robert Diaz, thank you for your most thoughtful work and talent in the design of this book. I appreciate the attention you gave to every detail, from layout to visual rhythm. Your work is part of how this book comes to life on the page in a beautiful story.

To the whole team at Clarkson Potter, including production editor Joyce Wong, production manager Jessica Heim, production designer Christina Self, editorial assistant Elaine Hennig, publicist Natalie Yera-Campbell, and marketer Joey Lozada, thank you for the dedication and countless hours behind the scenes to make this book possible. I'm thankful for each of you and the role you played in bringing these pages forward into the world in the best version possible.

To Julie Bishop, thank you for testing every recipe with such attention to detail. The thorough feedback you shared truly helped strengthen every recipe. I'm grateful for the time and endless dishes you poured into this and especially for your kind words that always seemed to arrive at the right time.

And, of course, I wouldn't be here without all of you—you reading this book, cooking my recipes, and sharing them with those you love. From the very first comment on my blog to every photo remake you've sent and each message you've written, your support has been the heartbeat of this journey. You've welcomed my food into your homes and onto your tables and, in doing so, made me feel like I've been a small part of your beautiful lives. This book exists only with your love, and my greatest hope is that when you cook from these pages, you feel the same love and joy that you've given me in return. Thank you a million times over and over.

INDEX

Note: Page references in *italics* indicate photographs.

D

E

Clarkson Potter/Publishers
An imprint of the Crown Publishing Group
A division of Penguin Random House LLC
1745 Broadway
New York, NY 10019
clarksonpotter.com
penguinrandomhouse.com

Library of Congress Cataloging-in-Publication Data
Names: Larbah, Hajar author | Kolenko, Eva photographer
Title: Moribyan's kitchen : 100 craveable comfort food recipes / Hajar Larbah ; photographs by Eva Kolenko.
Description: First edition. | New York : Clarkson Potter/ Publishers, [2026] | Includes index.
Identifiers: LCCN 2026002473 (print) | LCCN 2026002474 (ebook) |
ISBN 9798217034581 hardcover |
ISBN 9798217034598 ebook
Subjects: LCSH: Comfort food | Quick and easy cooking | Cooking, Moroccan | Cooking–Libya | LCGFT: Cookbooks
Classification: LCC TX714 .L3578 2026 (print) | LCC TX714 (ebook) | DDC 641.5/12–dc23/eng/20260129
LC record available at https://lccn.loc.gov/2026002473
LC ebook record available at https://lccn.loc.gov/2026002474

Hardcover ISBN 979-8-217-03458-1
Ebook ISBN 979-8-217-03459-8

Editor: Susan Roxborough
Editorial assistant: Elaine Hennig
Designer: Robert Diaz
Production editor: Joyce Wong
Production: Jessica Heim
Compositors: Merri Ann Morrell and Zoe Tokushige
Food stylist: Natalie Drobny
Food stylist assistant: Paige Arnett
Prop stylist: Genesis Vallejo
Copy editor: Eldes Tran
Proofreaders: Alisa Garrison and Hope Clarke
Indexer: Elizabeth Parson
Publicist: Natalie Yera-Campbell
Marketer: Joey Lozada

Printed in China

10 9 8 7 6 5 4 3 2 1

First Edition

The authorized representative in the EU for product safety and compliance is Penguin Random House Ireland, Morrison Chambers, 32 Nassau Street, Dublin D02 YH68, Ireland, https://eu-contact.penguin.ie.

Clarkson Potter/Publishers
An imprint of the Crown Publishing Group
A division of Penguin Random House LLC
1745 Broadway
New York, NY 10019
clarksonpotter.com
penguinrandomhouse.com

Library of Congress Cataloging-in-Publication Data
Names: Larbah, Hajar author | Kolenko, Eva photographer
Title: Moribyan's kitchen : 100 craveable comfort food recipes / Hajar Larbah ; photographs by Eva Kolenko.
Description: First edition. | New York : Clarkson Potter/Publishers, [2026] | Includes index.
Identifiers: LCCN 2026002473 (print) | LCCN 2026002474 (ebook) |
ISBN 9798217034581 hardcover |
ISBN 9798217034598 ebook
Subjects: LCSH: Comfort food | Quick and easy cooking | Cooking, Moroccan | Cooking–Libya | LCGFT: Cookbooks
Classification: LCC TX714 .L3578 2026 (print) | LCC TX714 (ebook) | DDC 641.5/12–dc23/eng/20260129
LC record available at https://lccn.loc.gov/2026002473
LC ebook record available at https://lccn.loc.gov/2026002474

Hardcover ISBN 979-8-217-03458-1
Ebook ISBN 979-8-217-03459-8

Editor: Susan Roxborough
Editorial assistant: Elaine Hennig
Designer: Robert Diaz
Production editor: Joyce Wong
Production: Jessica Heim
Compositors: Merri Ann Morrell and Zoe Tokushige
Food stylist: Natalie Drobny
Food stylist assistant: Paige Arnett
Prop stylist: Genesis Vallejo
Copy editor: Eldes Tran
Proofreaders: Alisa Garrison and Hope Clarke
Indexer: Elizabeth Parson
Publicist: Natalie Yera-Campbell
Marketer: Joey Lozada

Printed in China

10 9 8 7 6 5 4 3 2 1

First Edition

The authorized representative in the EU for product safety and compliance is Penguin Random House Ireland, Morrison Chambers, 32 Nassau Street, Dublin D02 YH68, Ireland, https://eu-contact.penguin.ie.

CLARKSON POTTER/PUBLISHERS
NEW YORK
CLARKSONPOTTER.COM

COVER DESIGN: ROBERT DIAZ
COVER PHOTOGRAPHS: EVA KOLENKO